Poverty, Gender, and Human Development

Context-Effective Cooperative Approaches

Poverty, Gender, and Human Development

Context-Effective Cooperative Approaches

A.H. Somjee
Professor Emeritus
Simon Fraser University

and

Geeta Somjee
Adjunct Professor of Political Science
Simon Fraser University

de Sitter Publications

CANADIAN CATALOGUING IN PUBLICATION DATA

POVERTY, GENDER, AND HUMAN DEVELOPMENT:
CONTEXT-EFFECTIVE COOPERATIVE APPROACHES
A.H. Somjee and Geeta Somjee

ISBN 0-9733978-8-8

Cover design: de Sitter Publications
Front cover: Photo taken by the authors. Design by de Sitter Publications.

de Sitter Publications
104 Consumers Dr., Whitby, ON, L1N 1C4, Canada

www.desitterpublications.com
sales@desitterpublications.com

PRINTED IN CANADA

Dedicated to the milk producers of India who, through their cooperative effort, achieved the impossible.

CONTENTS

CONTENTS

ACKNOWLEDGEMENTS

Given the prolonged duration of our study, it is difficult to remember and thank all those institutions and individuals who helped us. The two towering leaders who launched the dairy revolution in India, as stated earlier, were Dr. V. Kurien and the late Tribhuvandas Patel (TK). They gave us several hours of their time, year after year, to understand the complexities and dynamics of the evolving cooperative movement. Together with Dr. Amrita Patel, and a large number of socially concerned dairy technologists in the National Dairy Development Board (NDDB), they brought about significant changes in rural India where they operated. Remarkably, mainly small and marginal farmers and also landless laborers managed this alternative form of economic initiative. In a literal sense, this cooperative movement was sustained by the poor and neglected of rural India. By the year 2000, it had touched the lives of 60 million people. Further, its participatory mode of operation also enabled them to address other concerns, namely, health, gender distance, and the lack of opportunity for human development in general.

We wish to thank Dr. S.N. Singh, Dr. N.V. Belawadi, and G.P. Vijaya for their help in understanding the two crucial programs (Community Development and Women's Empowerment) launched by the NDDB.

Among the organizers of major milk cooperatives we wish to thank the following. In Amul Dairy: Dr. H.M. Dalaya, Dr. A. Chothani, Rahul Kumar Srivastava and the late Prafullabhai Bhatt. In Dudhsagar Dairy: Motibhai Chaudhury, B.C. Bhatt, Madhubhai Chaudhuri, Dr. A.S. Dave and Dr. D.P. Parmar. In SUMUL Dairy: P.R. Patel, Dr. H.A. Ghasia and Dr. Dilip Shah. In Vasudhara Dairy: Moghabhai Desai, Vashibhai, Suresh Desai and Bina Desai. In Sabar Dairy: Mayur Vyas and in Banas Dairy Sangramsingh Chaudhury. In Gokul Dairy: Dr. A. Wayangankar and Dr. D.V. Ghanekar. For dairies in Bihar we thank Dr. Punjarath, Amir Subhani, Dr. P.K. Sinha, Dr. P.N. Roychaudhury, and Dr.

Nadiadwala. Finally, for dairies in Rajasthan we thank Dr. Sudhir Varma and Premji Satsanghi.

We benefited immensely by the insights of Dr. Madhavan, Dr. R.K. Nair, Mr. Paramshivam, Dr. R.S. Daniel, Dr. Lester Nunes concerning the milk cooperative movement in Southern India.

Thanks are also due to Shastri Indo-Canadian Institute for a fellowship awarded to Geeta Somjee in 1994-95, for field research in women and development in rural India.

We wish to thank Brian Langdeau of Simon Fraser University, for his assistance in computer related work. We wish to thank Kishore Udaiver for his help with currency conversion. At the time when this manuscript was going to press, U.S.$1.00 was equal to RS. 45.00. Finally, we would like to express our sense of gratitude to Mr. Keith Povey for his help with copyediting our manuscript. We alone are responsible for any shortcomings in this volume.

A.H. Somjee and Geeta Somjee
Simon Fraser University

FOREWORD

Paul Steeten

A cartoon in *The New Yorker* showed two cows standing on the side of a highway. A giant truck passes. On it is written in large, colored letters: "pasteurized, rehydrated, biodynamic, reinforced, homogenized, vitamin-strengthened, reconstituted, purified milk." One of the sad-faced cows turns to the other and says, "To think that all this comes from us!" The cartoon illustrates the relationship between the practical, down-to-earth, pragmatic field workers and the grand, if not grandiose, writers in the development industry. A.H. and Geeta Somjee are, if they will forgive the comparison, like these two cows. They keep their noses well to the ground and gather the basic material that is then processed, and sometimes misinterpreted, into grand theories. And it is not a coincidence that their work has been concerned with the milk cooperatives of the poor in India.

The Somjees tell the fascinating story of the growth of Anand in the state of Gujarat, now the center of the Indian dairy cooperatives. The Amul (Anand Milk Union Limited) dairy covered almost all the thousand villages in the district by the mid-70s. It is an outstandingly successful marketing cooperative of small farmers and landless laborers, whose growth has been well documented by Geeta Somjee and A. H. Somjee. The Anand pattern was later replicated in other states of India under the name of Operation Flood, with the organizing genius of Verghese Kurien and his colleagues. It covered 75,000 village cooperatives, benefiting more than 55 million small and poor farmers and landless laborers, many of them women and members of lower castes. The Somjees' conclusion is that it is from experiences such as these that the lessons for development practitioners should be drawn, not from the arid models of some academic theorist.

The widening and deepening of the concept of poverty to include dimensions of deprivation, in addition to income, owes much to the work of the Somjees. These include social inferiority (social exclusion), isolation, vulnerability, powerlessness, and humiliation. In this attractive and elegantly argued book, A.H. Somjee and Geeta Somjee present a convincing picture of the links between poverty, gender, participation, and human development. And they thereby contribute to the fight for the reduction of poverty in all its dimensions.

Paul Streeten is Professor Emeritus of Boston University. He was a Professor of Economics and the Director of the World Development Institute at Boston University, and he has been a Professorial Fellow at Balliol College, Oxford and Warden of Queen Elizabeth House, Oxford. Dr. Streeten has worked closely with the World Bank and the Ministry of Overseas Development in the U.K. His ideas have influenced a large number of scholars in developed and developing countries, and a number of international development agencies around the world.

Poverty, Gender, and Human Development

An Introduction

People in developing countries have suffered, and continue to suffer, from poverty, illiteracy, inadequate health services, gender discrimination, lack of participation in the political process, and inadequate human development in general. The absence of an effective solution to these problems has compounded problems in other major areas such as economic growth, social equality, and good governance. Initially, many developing nations looked to their state institutions to solve their problems. However, apart from a handful of exceptions, such as in the countries of North and South East Asia, these institutions, in the absence of committed leadership and/or democratic pressure from below, delivered precious little. Many institutions lacked the political will to support bold policies or were victims of self-serving politicians and bureaucrats. Given such a situation they needed, and still do, alternative forms of public action to step in and bring about changes in few segments of the economy and society to begin with, and then move on to wider areas.

That is precisely what happened in some parts of rural India. While India remained mired in inefficiency and inaction from the 1960s to the 1980s, its cooperative dairy movement, which had an impact far beyond the dairy industry itself, was able to provide an alternative form of public action in some regions and sectors of its rural economy.

The organizers of the movement designed highly pragmatic schemes to make use of the available physical and human resources. They concentrated on India's enormous cattle wealth and improved upon it with the help of a new breed of research scientists and dairy technologists, and employed freshly graduated business administrators and marketing managers to get the best possible return for milk producers. Then they brought into the development equation the most neglected human resource, namely, women. Increasing participation by women opened up further opportunities for them in the areas of health, hygiene, and education. But these milk cooperatives did not stop there. They persuaded social activists in various regions to give them a helping hand in building and running participatory institutions at the grassroots level. For their part, the activists were happy to be given the opportunity to serve the newly established institutions, which were likely to make a difference to the condition of the poor and neglected. These interrelated, context-effective measures, as we shall see in this volume, created opportunities for further development in related fields.

In developing countries, among other things, three major areas have been identified where remedial action is urgently needed: rural poverty, gender inequality, and human development. It is believed that if these can be addressed simultaneously, they may stimulate improvements in other vital areas, such as economic growth, public participation, and responsive government.

Historically, and to varying degrees, all the countries of the world have in some measure experienced the problem of poverty. Developed countries, in particular, were able to reduce poverty by accelerating the pace of their economic growth. Accelerated growth rates created job opportunities and thus absorbed more and more jobless people into the workforce. But this took time. As Paul Patrick Streeten (1995) explains, "it took Britain 60 years to double real income per head after 1780; America 50 years after 1840; Japan 35 years after 1885; Turkey 20 years after 1957; Brazil 18 years after 1961; South Korea 11 years after 1966; and China 10 years after 1977" (pp.19-20). As a rule, therefore, countries that were able to double their real income, and go beyond it, were also able to reduce the level of poverty.

In Asia, those countries that managed to overcome the ravages of World War II, the lack of economic growth and poverty did so through a similar approach. In Japan, Singapore, Taiwan, and later South Korea, for instance, the absence of pressure from feudal interests, trade unions, and civil society enabled the state to adopt a somewhat authoritarian stance on development. Later, a corresponding approach was adopted by Malaysia, Indonesia, Thailand, and China. In all of these countries, while the market mechanism was allowed to operate so as to attract foreign investment, the state had virtually become a developmental state.

Such developmental states, however, did not neglect a *broader* approach to development. In all of these Asian countries whose economies began to register an impressive growth rate, pulling more and more people out of poverty, there was also an emphasis on what the World Bank Report (1993) called the "two-track approach," which involved investment both in economic growth and in people, by means of education, improved health care, employment, provision for housing and so on.

Jean Dreze and Amartya Sen came to a similar conclusion in their *India: Economic Development and Social Opportunity*. They faulted India for having neglected the broad social development of its people, excepting in certain states, while putting emphasis on economic growth. The result was that its economic growth did not register as fast a rate as was possible (Dreze and Sen 1995:81).

Those Asian countries that were able to accelerate their economic growth, however, also paid a price in other areas. Out of the three crucial choices to be made—economic growth, social and economic equality, and public participation in policy making— those countries that opted for the first had difficulty introducing even a minimum level of public participation. This was particularly true of South Korea and Taiwan for a long time. China initially opted for the second alternative, namely, social and economic equality, but then turned its attention to economic growth. All of them systematically avoided the third choice: public participation. Only

India among the Asian countries opted for it, albeit at the detriment of the other two. Samuel Huntington and Joan Nelson have argued about such choices, their consequences, irreversibility, nemeses of neglect, and so on, in those countries, with winners and losers in certain fields. To some extent the choices of these countries were determined by historical forces, nevertheless, they could have tried to bring in whatever they had missed out on. What most of them ended up having was a compromise between what they thought was normatively desirable and what was pragmatically possible (Huntington and Nelson 1987).

Poverty

India has the world's largest number of poor people. In recent years, however, it has made some progress in reducing poverty. But there is difficulty in measuring the extent of its achievement. Writing in *The New York Times*, Celia W. Dugger states that: "By nearly any economic measure, India is a poor country, but precisely how poor? The attempt to answer that question has sparked a vigorous debate in recent months among some of the country's leading economists" (Dugger October 8, 2000). Depending on one's methodology, the estimate of the poor below the poverty line in India ranged from 24.4 percent to 39.9 percent. Private research organizations found the most optimistic numbers of 18 percent below poverty line.

India's growth rate ranged from 2 to 4 percent during the four decades after independence, so it was not able to lift many of its poor out of poverty. In addition, the bulk of the poor were located in rural areas, where the problem of poverty was compounded with those caused by the hierarchically ordered traditional society. Poverty alleviation in this situation therefore needed a different approach that could address a mix of class and social hierarchy at the ground level.

Such an approach was spearheaded by India's milk cooperative movement with the help of a semi-nongovernmental organization called the National Dairy Development Board of India (NDDB). To a great extent it was able to keep self-serving bureaucrats and politicians at bay as its initial funding came from various international development agencies. Later on it was able to generate its own funds, which not only enabled it to remain independent of the government but also finance its own expansion into other regions. Over the years, given the variety of experiments in its regional units, and also demands from consumers and other organizations, it has been forced to go beyond milk in its various undertakings.

The work of the milk cooperative movement was premised on the assumption that since land was limited, it could not be given to everyone, not even with the help of the most radical land tenure policy. But people could be given, up to a point, other means to help them earn a small income to supplement what they already had. The other means in this case were milch animals. Such animals were a part of India's existing resources but required improvement in terms of quality and productivity. In such an exercise India's emerging scientific pool and dairy technologists could give a helping hand, as could the new breed of business and marketing managers. Moreover if women, who were already involved in the dairy industry, were brought in to take up responsible positions in decision-making bodies, the result might be even better. Finally, in all these exercises, nothing would ensure better supervision and results than the active participation of milk producers themselves. If they get involved then they would secure better performance from their organizers. That is what the NDDB did in order to put to effective use the available, and emerging, social and economic resources of India.

There are 596 districts in India and the milk cooperative movement has been able to establish its institutions in more than half of them. In 2001, it had a grassroots membership of more than 11 million people. If this number is multiplied by the average size of rural households (5.5), the movement has touched the lives of more than 60 million people. In 2001-2002, India had produced 84 million metric tons of milk. That amount has been rising at the rate of 7 percent per year. These cooperatives, in a span of 57 years, have now made India the largest milk producing country in the world.

What is remarkable about the cooperatives is that they are mostly managed by women. Furthermore, they are run on *democratic* lines, which has reinforced the democratic element in other grassroots institutions. But these cooperatives are not only about milk. Within them there are the dimensions of economic growth, opportunities to escape from poverty, concern for human health, nibbling away at gender distance, and learning to put democratic pressure on decision-makers at all levels to attend to other problems of the rural poor. This last exercise is central to the growth of their political capacity, with significance for wider human development.

Hence, the impact of the cooperatives has been multifaceted, but its major contribution has been to economic growth. Roughly 600 to 800 village cooperatives make up what is known as a milk union, and the most successful of these plough back into the district economy a sum ranging from Rs.400 to 700 crores or U.S.$88 million to U.S.$155 million.

The generation of such an income by the landless and marginal and small farmers is indeed a remarkable achievement. It has also encouraged a variety of new economic initiatives on the part of milk producers. Not only has it improved the economic conditions of farmers, it has also changed in most areas the nature of the district economy. The funds generated by milk, after deductions for routine and occasional expenses, have been used to experiment with cash crops, or to launch commercial ventures or small-scale industries in nearby towns.

This is what happened in Kheda district where India's famous Amul Dairy is located and which spearheaded the dairy revolution. The surplus funds generated by milk helped its rural entrepreneurs to experiment with cash crops, and even commercial and small-scale industrial ventures.

In Mehsana district, which incubated *mega* milk economies in its villages, the surplus funds generated by milk changed the nature

6

of the agricultural economy. The milk producers installed bore wells with the help of the additional cash. The availability of more water helped them sustain more milch animals, which in turn generated more cash. Thus the district was launched into an expanding dairy-agriculture-dairy cycle.

In the arid districts of north-western India, dairying became a *refuge* industry for farmers who could not continue with agriculture due to the failure of rainfall in their region. The two district milk cooperatives in that region, namely Sabar and Banas, opened up their doors to such farmers and helped them to keep their animals alive by giving them a steady income from milk, and also helped them with specially prepared cattle feed and fodder.

Then there were milk unions that helped to convert *adivasis* (tribals)—who had no milch animals worth the name and were not even an integral part of the mainstream society and economy—into milk producers. The Surat and Valsad districts brought the *adivasis* into the dairy community, which, in turn, helped them overcome their poverty and economic isolation.

In economically less developed states of India such as Rajasthan and Bihar, the income from milk cooperatives came as a great blessing to their small and marginal farmers who had to continue their agricultural work under highly adverse environmental and/or political conditions.

Hence the milk cooperatives, which had begun purely as institutions of milk producers, ended up becoming institutions to which the rural poor could turn for help in their other problems. As we shall see in this book, the membership of the milk cooperatives was increasingly drawn from small and marginal farmers, with 10 to 15 percent of them falling into the category of landless laborers, who are generally regarded as the poorest of the poor in India.

In terms of class and caste, over the years the milk producers seemed to fall into a *social queue*. In such a queue, the membership drawn from the upper class and castes began to dwindle and that from the OBCs (other backward communities), SCs (scheduled castes, including the former untouchables), STs (scheduled tribes) and the landless, who generally fell into the last two social categories, increased. In a genuine sense, then, these cooperatives had become institutions of small farmers or the "little guy."

However, the movement would not have got off the ground had it not been for social activists, who came from diverse backgrounds, had different professions and skills, and brought their own vision of what a cooperative movement should be. While their ideas had to be adapted to suit the local social and economic conditions, the most successful of them left behind their own clear imprints.

The two premier milk cooperatives—Amul in Anand and Dudhsagar in Mehsana—were the offshoots of the Indian national movement. What went into building them, in terms of human quality and dedication, was precisely what made the massive national movement possible. Moreover some of the top-flight leaders, both nationally and regionally, were their inspirers, and in some cases their founding fathers. Furthermore the qualities of the founding fathers rubbed off on the technocrats and technical personnel whom they later employed. As these personnel in turn trained managers and field workers in the grassroots organizations, the vision and message of the founding fathers was passed right down the line.

Given that the vast majority of farmers subsisted on meager or virtually no resources, very few technical personnel and social activists could resist the pull of those who needed their help. Just to be there, in any capacity, convinced them that there was *something* they could do or give that would make a difference, and strong bonds were soon formed with those they were helping. The movement also benefited immensely from Christian missionary organizations, which did remarkable work in organizing cooperatives in tribal areas.

Last but not least was the emergence of grassroots leaders. In the few fortunate communities where such leaders emerged, the latter's deep understanding of local problems enabled them to induct a larger number of poor into the milk-producing community. No social activist from outside could match their performance.

Narrowing the Gender Divide

Historically speaking women have been differently perceived in different cultures, and some of these cultures have also given their own justifications for subjecting women to certain disadvantages and inequalities (Ardener 1978). Despite improved education and social changes these justifications couched in religious, biological and/or economic terms have continued to influence, to varying degrees, the attitude of men and society towards women.

At various conferences and meetings of learned societies, a question often asked is whether the approaches adopted by the various feminist groups and women's liberation movements in western countries, with their emphasis on women's *empowerment,* are suited to women in non-western countries. It is increasingly being recognized that while women in many parts of the world face similar disadvantages, the solution to them, given women's historical and cultural diversity, has to be different. For instance, the anti-male stance of many western feminist theories, albeit to varying degrees, does not carry much weight in developing countries such as India, where men have also played an important part in whatever advances women have made. Furthermore it is realized, both by women and by men supporting women's causes, that it is not enough to make provisions in law and policy to remove women's social disadvantages, but also persuade them to get involved in the various social and political movements that influence their enactment. This will give them a much better appreciation of the progress that has been made so far, and what still needs to be done. But more than that, women need to grow in their political capacity, which they can only do by involving themselves in political processes that aim at specific targets to benefit them (Somjee 1989).

One of the finest examples of such involvement is again provided by the Indian milk cooperative movement. The founding fathers of the cooperatives knew that women would be central to their effort. However their and their successors' perception of the role of women gradually evolved from women as the real managers of the milk economy to their being more pliable and less political and therefore no harm in having them inside the organizations. For their part women welcomed the opportunity to become involved when the cooperatives came to their doorstep and promised additional income for them and their families.

Conceptually speaking, the perception of the cooperatives towards women evolved in the following manner. Initially they treated women as *targets,* whereby the expectation was to involve more of them in different aspects of the dairy industry of which they were the unacknowledged managers in any case. So it was logical to pass on more work to them. Later such a view gave way to treating women as *conduits* through which various changes in domestic cowshed could be implemented. The artificial insemination drive, the massive switch to crossbred cows, and animal healthcare were generally routed through women. Simultaneously, there was also an emphasis on the involvement of women because men were perceived as less compliant to the policies of the organizers than were women. Furthermore women were seen as less interested in treating milk cooperatives as a stepping-stone to the fulfillment of larger political ambitions or goals than men.

Throughout their explorations into what an appropriate role for women should be, the goal of the organizers remained the same: to increase milk production. Without involving themselves in any ambitious attempt to overcome the gender divide, the organizers wanted women as allies on their side in their pursuit of greater productivity and procurement. Very few of them expected women to grow in their participatory or political capacity, and then turn around and make a few demands of their own. The organizers did not think of women as emerging into, what we have called, *critical agents,* who would not only become crucial to the running of the cooperatives but would also put forward demands of their own. In other words, as critical agents there would be no knowing what they would demand next.

The organizers' attitude towards women remained ambivalent. While they wanted the glory of helping women to become active members of the cooperatives and to help raise productivity, they also expected women to side with them against squabbling men, and above all to help prevent men from using cooperative institutions to further their political ambitions. However when women did emerge as critical agents and began to make certain demands of their own, the organizers were secretly delighted to have emboldened and empowered them enough to reach that stage. Such an evolution of women, from targets to conduits to critical agents, is central to our understanding of their ethnopolitical development.

The emergence of women as critical agents in certain states was further accelerated by a massive management and leadership training program launched by the NDDB. Its logic was simple. Since dairying was increasingly becoming gender specific, it was only fair that women should receive training in its management and leadership. Such a training, coming on top of women's increasing involvement in participatory processes of cooperatives, further advanced their social and political capacity. In Chapter 3 we shall illustrate this with examples from various states.

Human Development

During the last twenty years there has been a sea change in the thinking of development economists and they have gradually begun to acknowledge that there is much more to development than economic growth. While economic growth remains the very foundation of development, as it provides the wherewithal for services such as education, health care, and so on, such services also ensure continued economic growth. That is, the two stand in a symbiotic relationship with one another, with each stimulating and benefiting the other. This has been demonstrated by the World Bank (1993), and by Jean Dreze and Amartya Sen (1995). The former argues that the countries of East Asia enjoyed high economic growth because they attended to literacy, healthcare and other human requirements, while the latter argue that because India ignored such provisions its economic growth was poor.

In *Thinking About Development* (1995), Paul Streeten argues that human development is not a "new fad," but the product of a gradual change in economists' thinking on development. They arrived at it "from economic growth, via employment, jobs and justice, redistribution with growth, to basic needs, finally to human development" (Streeten 1995:19-20). For Streeten it was far more inclusive, extending to poverty eradication, economic growth, family planning, education, health, civil society, political participation and so on.

Starting with a general criticism of the World Bank for neglecting in its annual reports the human dimensions of development, Mahbub ul Haq argues that the time has come to replace national income with human well-being as the principal concern of development:

> The basic purpose of development is to enlarge people's choices. In principle, these choices can be infinite and can change over time. People often value achievements that do not show up at all, or not immediately, in incomes or growth figures. [This may include] greater access to knowledge, better nutrition and health services, more secure livelihood, security against crime and physical violence, satisfying leisure hours, political and cultural freedoms and a sense of participation in community activities. The objective of development is to create an enabling environment for people to enjoy long, healthy and creative lives. (Haq 1995:14)

Both Streeten and Haq thus put *human beings* into the development equation and maintain that there is much more to their development than national income and its distribution. Both take a neo-Kantian position that views humans as ends in themselves rather than simply means to boost economic growth and national strength. Both thus share the highly respectable intellectual position taken by scholars as diverse as Aristotle, Immanuel Kant, Adam Smith, John Stuart Mill, and Karl Marx.

Haq, in particular, is conscious of the fact that economists have become receptive to the idea of going beyond economic indicators when discussing development. He has therefore formulated what he calls a "paradigm" of development to widen its appeal. Two sides of human development are emphasized: "the formation of human capabilities—such as improved health, knowledge and skills. The other is the use of...acquired capabilities—for employment, productive activities, political affairs or leisure" (Haq 1995:13-14).

While Haq admits that cultural factors, peculiar to each society, have to be taken into account when discussing human development, he does not pay special attention to some of the hierarchically ordered societies that devastate their lower strata. In their case the provision of services for education and skills is not enough to stimulate human development. What is also needed is a participatory process in which they can restore their sense of self-worth as human beings in the first place.

In India's hierarchically ordered society those who were regarded as untouchables were made to feel inferior through adroit use of "*karmic rationale*" by its upper castes. Since the untouchables were a source of cheap agricultural labor, the upper castes always made the point that it was the *karma* of the untouchables in their past life that had made them what they were, and therefore they should not blame the upper castes who employed them. More than three thousand years of recorded history of Indian civilization had caused the former untouchables deeply to internalize those arguments, so when they were offered opportunities, through various affirmative programs and policies, they just could not make full use of them. For a long time thereafter they needed social activists to guide them to various policy provisions, and they still do today.

What was more the social activists, and the woefully slow leadership of the downtrodden, were by themselves not good enough to build back their sense of self-worth. The socially disadvantaged also needed social and economic involvement in the broader community of which they were a part, to restore their confidence and rejuvenate them as human beings. They needed to be deeply convinced that they too were a vital part of their society as any other individual within it. For this to be brought about the initial affirmative measures had to be followed up by an access to equality of opportunity. While the various national and local electoral processes, for constituting various political authorities, did provide some participatory opportunities, it was difficult for them to realize their own empowerment through such processes. What in fact, helped them much more, not only in the growth of their political capacity but also in their *ethnodevelopment* in general, were the participatory opportunities provided by the milk cooperative movement which came to their door step in various parts of India. By becoming actively involved in the cooperatives the socially disadvantaged, including former untouchables, and women, were offered a chance of self-development, and thereby gradually alter their traditional social and economic relationships which had condemned them to a status of inferiority and sub-humanity. The various chapters of this book provide grassroots images of how the socially disadvantaged in rural society were able to benefit from those opportunities. Some of those opportunities, at least initially, were not even intended to benefit them. It was merely a fortuitous combination of circumstances that brought the socially concerned dairy personnel and social activists of the region to help the disadvantaged to benefit from the participatory opportunities that had come to the grassroots communities.

The concept of human development thus needs to be looked at not only from the perspective of policy and provision for services, but also from the point of view of involving in participatory processes those who are, or have been, socially and economically disadvantaged. This is because if disadvantaged groups are made mere recipients of what is legislated for them, their political capacity does not increase. Active involvement in the political process is essential for them to become demanders and takers of what may be deemed rightfully theirs.

The process of growing to full selfhood in a community of participating individuals will also ensure that they will look at development opportunities in the same way as others do in their community—similar to the universal adult franchise which provides everyone with equal voting opportunity. In this case, equal development opportunity to take your rightful place in a community where everyone is expected to benefit by means of equality of opportunity. For this some prior groundwork—by way of education, affirmative action policies, and socially concerned individuals initially guiding them—will be necessary. But once through those stages, there is a possibility of such individuals coming into their own, like any other member of society. Of course there are some among them who would like to be perennial wards, but limited duration of affirmative policies should be able to check that.

The participatory process introduced by the grassroots cooperatives, which was also tied up with the livelihood of the average milk producer, made involvement a serious business and transformed it from a desirable ideal to a social and economic necessity.

Chapter 1

Creating New Resources for the Neglected

It is often believed that a high tide of economic growth can lift all countries, big and small, out of poverty. Such a tide, however, cannot be made to order. Nor can countries with a large proportion of poor among them wait indefinitely for one to arrive. They have to devise alternative ways of helping their people escape poverty.

A high tide of economic growth was noticeable in recent years in countries such as South Korea, Taiwan, Singapore, Malaysia, Thailand, and Indonesia. They created conditions to attract foreign investment, ruthlessly suppressed social and political forces that challenged the power of the state, and provided health and educational services to their people in order to improve their skills. In the consequent economic development of those countries, therefore, both internal and external forces have played a part. Also accompanying them have been the geopolitical forces, the changing nature of international trade, revolution in the transportation industry, and, above all, result-oriented public policies. Behind their high tide of economic growth, therefore, many internal and external forces are evident.

A large number of developing countries, including India, for a variety of reasons, were not as fortunate. Such countries were left to their own devices. Consequently, India made ingenious use of its own natural and human resources to help a segment of its people rise above poverty.

In most developing countries poverty is concentrated in rural areas. Since land is limited, it cannot be distributed to everyone. Up to a point, however, most of them can create alternative means to generate income for their poor. Such means differ from country to country. In the Indian context, the most effective alternative means for the rural poor are the milch animals. That was precisely what the burgeoning milk cooperatives of India did in order to supplement the income of the poor and transform the economy of the rural districts to benefit them still further.

Started as an institution for procuring, processing and marketing milk for the "milk producers," regardless of their caste and class, Indian milk cooperatives soon penetrated into the lower strata of India's traditional social organization. In response to their efforts, some kind of a social queue appeared in different parts of the country. The upper castes and classes were the first to participate. But they did not always find returns from their investment in cattle very attractive. Consequently, they became indifferent to dairying. The next to come to the forefront were, what is called in acronyms, the OBCs (Other Backward Classes). In some parts of the state of Gujarat, where cooperative dairying originated, they built a mega milk economy for the district. Lower castes and *dalits* (the former untouchables), with small pieces of land, then followed the OBCs. The last to join the queue were the *adivasis* (tribals) who were the poorest of the poor. Cooperative dairying in India thus became, unlike in the United States, Australia, New Zealand, and Canada, an undertaking by small farmers. But these small farmers with their combined efforts built something much bigger than anybody could have imagined.

In a span of fifty years the cooperative movement, largely based in the lower economic strata of rural society, unleashed what the World Bank described as, "the Dairy Revolution" (World Bank Report 1993). The impact of it was felt far beyond the milk economy. For one thing it generated more cash than was expected. That in turn stimulated, in certain parts of India, cash crops and new economic initiatives. The movement also inducted more women into the economy and provided them with the opportunity for participating in decision-making processes that affected their well-being. Its impact was thus many-sided.

In 1998, the people of India learned with some disbelief that their country had overtaken the United States in milk production and had occupied the first place in the world. That achievement was considered to be unique because despite its potential to make a mark in several fields, India had, in fact, achieved precious little in its half century of existence as an independent country. During the same period, its record in the field of literacy, poverty, sanitation, clean water, housing, and so on, had been deplorable. And yet what was achieved in the field of dairying, in quantitative as well as qualitative terms along with its impact, was indeed a major event. For it was not just the quantity of milk produced, but who produced it, and to what effect, that was equally important. And what was more, these milk producers, by and large, were small and marginal farmers who did not own much land. All across India, more and more landless farm workers, by claiming farm cuttings as a part of their daily wage, were also able to join the grassroots milk producing communities and supplement their income.

This chapter is divided into the following subsections: (I) The Burgeoning Milk Economy; (II) Milk Liquidity and its Impact; (III) Mega Milk Communities; (IV) Overcoming Environmental Limitations; (V) Taking Cooperatives to the Tribals; (VI) Benefiting from Urban Linkages; (VII) Milk Cooperatives with Difficult Beginnings; and finally (VII) Some General Observations.

I. The Burgeoning Milk Economy

The milk cooperatives, as an alternative form of economic undertaking, simultaneously worked in two directions. It inducted more and more people with little or no resources into the dairy industry, and also generated a surplus of cash, sometimes huge, enabling milk producers to diversify their economic undertakings. The savings from milk supported not only experiments in cash crops, but also commercial ventures in district towns. In some district towns, such savings were even helpful in starting small industrial units. In many rural districts of India, where the milk economy has flourished, there are now many prosperous district towns. The sheer size of the operation of milk cooperatives in certain districts and states should give us some idea of the extent of their influence on the economic and social life of the people. This we shall illustrate in this chapter.

Approximately half of the 596 plus districts in India now have set up milk cooperatives in their villages. The full magnitude of this achievement became clear when its principal architect, Dr. Verghese Kurien —the builder of Amul Dairy, and the one who shouldered the mighty task of launching and consolidating the milk cooperative movement itself— decided to retire in 1998 after 50 years of distinguished service. When tributes started coming in from various quarters, one was able to get a glimpse of all that had been achieved.

An article in the *Economic Times of India*, 18 October 1998, stated the following: "There are 10 million families (1998) in the country who are involved in milk producing. These families are organized into 75,000 village cooperatives who own 170 modern cooperative dairy plants, which form part of 22 state marketing federations." This was, indeed, a staggering achievement. And if we multiply the 10 million milk producing families (in 2002 they reached the figure 11 million) by 5.5, which is roughly the size of an average rural family in India, Kurien and his colleagues had provided an additional income to more than 60 million people.

Meanwhile, a news item in *the Hindu*, 16 October 1998, reported that "the country's milk yield increased from 20 million tons to over 70 million tons per annum under the Operation Flood program in the last 20 years, generating an additional rural income of Rs.50,000 crores against an investment of Rs.100 crores. Since the additional income had accrued mainly to the womenfolk, the money earned had been spent more for the welfare of the family, improving the living standard of the small and marginal farmers in rural India."

Finally, in the words of Professor Katar Singh, of the Institute of Rural Management in Anand (IRMA), the Indian milk cooperative movement had become "the largest network of agribusiness co-cooperative in the world" (Katar Singh 1996).

Let us now consider, in rupee terms, how much money some of the major milk unions have poured into their districts' economy when they purchased milk from villages and sold it to towns and cities. In that sense, these cooperative institutions were involved in keeping the rural population in the countryside itself and giving it cash returns at its own locations.

Not all milk cooperatives retained their preeminent role in building the economy of the district over a long period of time. That had much to do with their resources, leadership, and the experimenting disposition of the milk producers themselves.

Historically speaking, the milk cooperatives of Gujarat, which launched "the Dairy Revolution" in India, were also supported by several grassroots movements and social activists. In some districts of Gujarat, the milk cooperative movement was literally an offshoot of the Indian national movement, which had emphasized a *cooperative approach* as a part of its broader strategy to discard goods and services coming from abroad during the colonial period. The milk cooperatives, however, did not stop there. As they went ahead with their enterprises, they also brought in state-of-the-art dairy technology, professional management, modern marketing skills, etc., all of this without giving up their concern for the milk producers in rural areas. Over the years, their commitment to milk producers also persuaded them to explore the possibility of inducting those who were either economically backward and/or socially disadvantaged. The ultimate challenge was to include even the landless. And there, too, they had an increasing measure of success. Nearly three quarters of cooperative membership was drawn from milk producers who were either small or marginal farmers. Then there was an increasing number of landless who also became members. They did this by making farm cuttings a part of their wages. To that they added specially prepared cattle feed.

Depending on the region one went to, there was increasing evidence of more money coming into the village economy. Some of the villages in Gujarat, albeit limited in number, literally became what we have called "*mega* milk villages," with income from milk alone in 2004 ranging from Rs.1 crore (U.S.$222,222) to Rs.6 crores (U.S.$1.3m). This did not include their agricultural income. We watched some of those villages in different districts over a period of twenty-five years, and also kept track of joint families who had diversified their income by undertaking commercial ventures in nearby towns or sent their children to cities to pursue higher education and get professional degrees. The liquidity generated by milk thus acted as an *enabling* factor making it possible for people to go beyond milk in their economic enterprise. In some districts, the more successful milk producers either reduced their dairy herd or opted out of the milk economy altogether. This was particularly true, as we shall see, of the economically enterprising caste of Patidars in the district of Kheda.

II. Milk Liquidity and its Impact

The five premier milk cooperatives in Gujarat rose to prominence largely through grassroots efforts and poured huge amounts of money into the rural communities. These were the milk unions of Amul, Dudhsagar, Sumul, Sabar, and Banas. A milk union normally consists of 800 to 1,000 village milk cooperatives. There was competition among these premier milk cooperatives and their managers often worried about keeping it within healthy limits (i.e., they did not want their public pronouncements about each other to go beyond productivity figures and the quality of service provided). The only competition they did not welcome was from the multinationals with their worldwide connections and concessions extracted not only from their home base but also from the host country, i.e., India.

The milk cooperative movement, which started with Amul in 1946, spread to the rest of the country. Before Amul there were a few attempts in different regions, but they did not get off the ground. Amul had perfected the model of a farmer–owned and operated milk cooperative. Such a model came to be known as the "Anand Pattern" cooperative because Amul (Anand Milk Union Limited) is located in a town called "Anand." Then under the Operation Flood, it was replicated elsewhere by the NDDB (National Dairy Development Board), also located in Anand. Such a pattern turned out to be the most feasible with an enormous significance for other compartments of rural life. The liquidity generated by Amul, through the sale of milk, has had an enormous impact on the city of Anand and its commercial and industrial development. The amount injected into Kheda district, where Amul is located, may not be very impressive by today's standard, but it certainly was adequate and timely, especially for those agriculturists who were making a switch from agriculture to commerce and/or industry.

In 1891, the township of Anand had a population of nine thousand people and was granted the status of an urban municipality. A century later it had grown into five hundred thousand people, and its sleepy little community, with its shopkeepers, carpenters, and blacksmiths, was transformed beyond recognition. Every time, the stimulus for change came from its rural hinterland. By the 1930s, one of its prosperous and innovative agriculturist communities, the Patidars (with Patel as their surname), began producing surplus grain. This was then brought into the market. But that was not enough for them. Their children, especially in their six socially prestigious villages, locally called the *mota gams*, started taking education, and sought employment opportunities in the former British colonies in Africa. This further added to their income. Some of them, on return, tried their hand at commercial undertakings in Anand but continued to hold on to their land. With the coming of independence, and the passage of the Land Tenancy Act, the Patidars lost to their tenants at least 10 percent of the land they owned. In order to get more out of the remaining land, they had to switch to cash crops such as tobacco, cotton, bananas, mustard, vegetables, limes, etc. Precisely at that juncture, Amul dairy was setting up more and more milk cooperatives. Given the availability of fodder on their land, the Patidars went into dairying in a big way. Their interest in it peaked in the 1990s, and then started to decline. In one of our earlier published works, we had described this as follows:

"One of the greatest single attractions to the Patidars to stay in agriculture, despite more attractive economic opportunities which the burgeoning town of Anand provided, was the absence of tax on agricultural income. And it is here that the extended nature of Indian family proved to be a great boon. The enterprising Patidar could ask his brother or cousin in the village to cultivate his land, with the help of agricultural labor, and then move into Anand with his own family so as to undertake commercial or industrial venture. What such extended families thus did was to diversify their own human resources to different forms of economic enterprise. So great was the benefit of such a diversification that every 'successful' farmer in the region was expected to back up the progression of one or more members of his family towards commerce or industry. While in undertaking such ventures a Patidar no doubt took some risk, nevertheless, he also had his land to fall back upon just in case the commercial or industrial venture did not succeed. The closely knit extended family, together with the facility for absentee agriculture, down in the village, provided to the Patidars a sense of security for new ventures."[1]

Apart from the added income from milk, the growth of the transport industry, stimulated by the dairy industry bringing cans of milk from its eight hundred plus milk cooperatives in villages, also helped the farmers send their crops to the markets in Anand, and through them, helped farmers reach major marketing centers in big cities by means of railroads and trucks. This, in turn, stimulated commercial activity in Anand. Stores selling textiles, shoes, bicycles, scooters, TVs, refrigerators, medical supplies, spare auto parts, etc., opened up, presenting increasing opportunities to farmers who wanted to diversify their sources of income. Then came people with various professional backgrounds. In the beginning there was an influx of teachers, doctors, lawyers, accountants, and engineers from outside Anand. Later on, the locally based educational institutions started meeting the demands for training in skills and professions. The next to follow in this chain was the small and medium scale industry. Starting from the outskirts of Anand, its industrial development stretched out over a radius of 20 miles from the city.

In such phenomenal growth of the district, the enterprising disposition of the Patidars had no doubt played an important part. They now were at the forefront of all three major economies of the district, namely, agriculture, commerce, and industry. Even in dairying, they were at the forefront of improvement in the milk yielding capacity of the animal. They were the first to switch to crossbred cows from the age-old, and much too familiar, buffalo. With their help, Amul, the flagship of India's dairy industry and the model for the rest of the country, enjoyed a preeminent position until the second half of the 1990s. In 1997 it even procured a million litres of milk per day during the peak production period, or what the locals called the flush season. It poured into the economy of the district large sums of money earned by means of the sale of milk. Moreover, most of this money went into its villages. The Patidars, at least in Kheda district, were at the center of it.

However, Amul's position then began to slip because of the loss of Patidars' interest in the milk economy. The Patidars who, in fact, were great diversifiers of sources of income, went in search of still new places to invest. And this time they hit upon the most unlikely source. They now wanted their children to take good education and settle abroad, so that they themselves could follow. If they could not follow them through the legitimate route, they went in search of what the locals called the *do number ka rasta* or the backdoor. There are now a large number of Patidars in Britain and the United States doing exceedingly well. The bulk of them have come through the legitimate route.

Dairying seemed a sufficiently respectable pursuit when the Patidars were an economically struggling group, but that had changed. Now, one of the ways of going abroad was to marry their daughters to boys who had settled abroad. Those would-be bride-grooms, according to some, did not like girls who had to look after cowsheds back home, as they reeked of it for the rest of their lives. So there was motivation to be rid of dairying and thus give their daughters a chance as brides of overseas Patidars.

Amul paid heavily for depending on the Patidars as the mainstay of dairying in the district. In the world of dairying, your prestige as a milk union is based on the quantity of milk you collect and, secondly, on the kind of policy that you put in place to benefit the weaker segments of your milk producing community. Unfortunately, Amul lost on both of those counts. In the late 1990s, it was deeply involved in painful introspection and finding a way out of the crisis. Other milk unions, as we shall presently see, which encouraged other social groups, escaped such a downturn. The districts of Mehsana, Sabar, Banas, Surat, Valsad, etc., all in Gujarat —which encouraged the Chaudhuries (OBCs), the Lower Castes (LCs), the Scheduled Castes (SCs), and Scheduled Tribes (STs), and not just Patidars and Desais—escaped such a decline. One could find similar examples in Karnataka and Tamil Nadu in the South, in Maharastra in the West and, to a limited extent, in Rajasthan and Bihar in the North. Still looking to the Patidars to bale it out, Amul was hoping that they may yet come back to dairy-ing provided profits were good enough. One of the ways of inducing them, again, was to interest them in an economy of scale. That is to say, persuade them to become big producers and benefit by the bulk sales and, in the end, even try out some form of milk capitalism. Very few Patidars, however, took that bait.

Amul persisted in its attempts to get back to its preeminent position as a milk producing and marketing union. In the spring of 2004, under the youthful leadership of Rahul Kumar Srivastava (an alumnus of IRMA (Institute of Rural Management), which had built its core curriculum round the special management requirements of rural institutions such as milk cooperatives), Amul tried a variety of approaches to reverse its declining fortunes. To continue and expand its stake in cooperative dairying, it began offering better returns to its milk producers. The prosperous consumers of the district of Kheda, where Amul is located, took the rising price of milk in stride. Subsequently, Amul employed the highly regarded veterinarians of neighboring districts to improve the quality of its animals. Its marketing staff was asked to pay more attention to what the urban consumer wanted by way of its milk products. For more than three decades, Amul, for instance, had restricted itself to making processed cheese. The middle-class consumers of India had enough of it. They now wanted more variety, in particular a cheese-base like Mozzarella to mix with a range of homemade dishes. For a long time Amul, given its near monopoly in cheeses, marketed mostly processed cheese. That was beginning to change.

Such changes, no doubt, began to improve the revenue of Amul, however, several nagging questions persisted: Was Amul able to renew its contact with the grassroots milk producing community? Did it succeed in gradually replacing the traditional milk producing community of the district, namely, the Patidars, by cultivating other agriculturist groups such as the OBCs, the SCs and others of the district? It was indeed difficult to tell.

Amul occupied its preeminent position for a long time and then started losing it to its own progeny, the Dudhsagar Dairy in the city of Mehsana. The latter, for a long time, called itself "the child of Amul," but in fact had excelled it both in milk procurement and the quality of its policies. Similarly, Sumul in Surat, Vasudhara in Valsad, Banas in Palanpur, Gokul in Kolhapur, and others started introducing a variety of programs to help their milk producing communities, the bulk of which came from the middle or lower rungs of rural society. All of them had one goal in common: to be better than Amul. Amul, nevertheless, as a brand name for quality (and a symbol of what farmers of India had achieved with the help of dairy scientists, veterinarians, professional managers, and marketing experts), survived. So did the mystique built round its name, "Amul," which in Indian languages means priceless. It also reminded the people of the best that had come out of milk producers' cooperative effort to improve their economic condition by providing quality products to urban consumers.

At the other extreme of such dairy dynamics, was Dudhsagar in the neighboring district of Mehsana. Located in a semi-arid district, where there was poor soil and equally poor quality of water, Dudhsagar, with the help of liquidity generated by milk, was able to change the face of that district. Twenty-five years ago we started going to Mehsana from Anand by jeep, and when we entered the district borders, we saw nothing but windswept dry land with a lot of weed around. Today, one sees in most of those areas nothing but greenery as a result of bore wells put in place with the help of money from milk. A good part of the liquidity generated by milk was put into agriculture first, which generated more greenery, which in turn was able to sustain more milch animals. Mehsana has thus become an expanding milk-agriculture-milk economy.

While Mehsana did not have good land, nor enough water, what it did have, nevertheless, were good animals and expert breeders called the Chaudhuries on the one hand, and a highly dedicated staff of veterinarians, dairymen, and managers who were deeply influenced by the Indian national movement itself, on the other. The dairy staff of Dudhsagar retained the idealism of the national movement even fifty years after independence. With the exception of some rural communities in Maharastra and Tamil Nadu, you rarely find people in charge of institutions showing such a depth of social concern. Since Dudhsagar came after Amul, it was also able to avoid some of its trial-and-error mistakes. Some of the mistakes committed by Amul, fell into two categories. First, when the organization became too big and too professional it gradually lost contact with the producers. Second, it failed to pay sufficient attention to the animal resources available in the region and the need to continually improve their productivity.

III. Mega Milk Communities

In a literal sense, Dudhsagar has turned the district of Mehsana into a mega milk economy. Since 1988 some of its villages have been earning large sums of money by selling milk.

In 2002-2003, Dudhsagar's top ten villages recorded the following amount of income from their sale of milk:

Village	Income		Population
	Rs.	U.S.$	
1. Charada 1&2	62671108.13	1.39m	9930
2. Pamol 1 &2	47162235.18	1.04	4650
3. Balva	49687387.25	1.10m	6144
4. Bapupura 1&2	42137684.00	935,554	2389
5. Indrapura	29348121.45	651,110	2065
6. Solaiya 1&2	35416398.00	786,66	3761
7. Kheralu	33207374.51	737,777	18632
8. Amja	17153454.92	379.99	2622
9. Rangakui	22276272.00	493,332	1577
10. Vithoda	22769536.74	505,989	2572

Source: Figures supplied by Dudhsagar Dairy.

What was equally remarkable about their milk producers was that the bulk of them were small and marginal farmers with an increasing number of landless laborers among them. Their membership was drawn from the landless (15.70 percent), marginal farmers (33.02 percent), small farmers (38.64 percent), and big farmers (12.64 percent). Even caste-wise, their membership was quite impressive. Their mainstay were the Chaudhuries, the well-known breeders of animals, until recently considered to be the OBCs. They were then followed by the BCs and STs. (Source: Figures supplied by Dudhsagar Dairy.)

There is healthy competition among the mega milk villages themselves. They wish to join, or move up on, the list of the honored top ten. Most of these villages are located in a subdistrict of Mehsana called *Mansa*. Mansa taluka, or subdistrict, has 61 villages that produce nearly 24 to 25 percent of Dudhsagar's total milk. And Dudhsagar Dairy, at the moment, is the topmost milk-producing dairy in India and in Asia. There is thus a kind of Asian and even global consciousness sweeping across the villages of Gujarat, especially if you have something to boast about.

Within Mansa subdistrict there is a village called Charada. At the moment it occupies the topmost position in the milk production chart in Dudhsagar. In 1998-1999, the village earned a staggering amount of Rs.3.51 crores (U.S.$779,999) from the sale of milk alone. Out of its total membership, 79 families have an income of above Rs.1 *lakh* (100,000 rupees or U.S.$2,222) per year from milk. A lakh of rupees, until recently, had the same significance in India as a million dollars in western countries. The bulk of Charada milk producers come from Chaudhury, local Patidar, Thakore, Scheduled Caste, and Vaghari communities, which are all classified as OBCs and below. Its membership is also drawn from small and marginal farmers and the landless.

Charada sent 400 cans of milk per day to Dudhsagar in 2001, and enjoyed a high standard of living. Half of the village households have TVs, and one-third possess refrigerators. There are 22 Jeeps in the village, 70 tractors, 12 Matador vans, and 7 Maruti cars. Finally, a number of households claim that they have close relatives in different parts of America and talk of New Jersey, Chicago, California, as if they were "next-door." There is one wrinkle, however, on this extremely rosy picture of Charada. The village of Balva has eclipsed Charada. With half of Charada's population, Balva's income per capita from milk is much higher than Charada's.

One of the most prestigious villages in the district, both for its productivity and social conscience, is Pamol. It was also one of the earliest to give a stunning performance in terms of milk productivity. Close to one-third of its population consists of Chaudhuries. And it was in this village that the Chaudhury women started working actively with veterinary research scientists, setting an example for women in other rural communities to follow. It was also in this village that the leaders developed a cooperative fodder farm on the village *gauchar* (village common) in order to help the landless own milch animals by working on the farm and getting wages and fodder at a reasonable rate. Within the district, Pamol has become a symbol of what the villagers themselves could do for their fellow poor. It has thus earned the reputation of being a compassionate village. During periods of drought in the neighboring districts, it always opened up its doors to drought migrants and their animals to tide over hard times. The migrants then worked on the fodder farm, got fodder at a reduced rate, and poured milk in the Pamol milk cooperative. Moreover, Pamol has not only its own veterinary hospital, but also hospitals for human beings, a cooperative bank, and a credit and lending society, which never lost a penny and has a saving balance of Rs.5 crores or U.S.$1.11m (1999) in the bank. We have watched this village over a period of twenty years.

In 1988-1989, Pamol earned an income of Rs.1.16 crores (U.S.$257,777) from its sale of milk. Ten years later, it tripled to Rs.3.49 crore (U.S.$775,554). That amount, for a village believed to be of 5,000 people, was very creditable. It is second to Charada in its income from milk with less than half of its population. Forty-one of its members earn above a *lakh* of rupees each year from milk.

Pamol's agricultural income continues to be half of its income from milk. Thus, the income from milk had far exceeded the income from land. For one thing, you cannot increase your landholding, but you can go on increasing the number of animals almost by as much as your capacity permits. And the farmers of Mehsana district have so far shown a preference for milk rather than agriculture or industrial diversification, as did the Kheda district where Amul is located.

The question, then, is where does that additional income go? The answer is as follows. There are now many *pucca* (brick or cement built) houses in the village with a lot of sophisticated indoor plumbing and amenities. The residents of Pamol no longer list TVs, refrigerators, scooters, and automobiles as something to boast about. Years ago they used to do that enthusiastically. Now they take for granted that those things are there with most people. They sometimes talk about washing machines, but mention that they do not have much use for them, as plenty of domestic help is available The bulk of additional income goes to their savings bank accounts for future use such as weddings, improvement of dwellings, experiments in cash crops, and starting commercial ventures in nearby towns.

They routinely deride urban living. It can be paraphrased as follows: "now we have everything that city dwellers have, without hassle and pollution. What we do not have, however, are good schools in nearby locations. And yet nearly 100 boys and girls go by bus to schools and colleges in nearby towns." Their emphasis on higher education for their children has risen as a result of the possibility of settling their educated children in America with prospects for parents to visit them there.

Pamol, however, is not without its competitors. The village Indrapura, which is also located in Mansa taluka, has only one-half of Pamol's population but it earned a whopping amount of Rs.2.56 crores (U.S.$568,888) in the year 1997-1998. Clearly, then, in terms of per capita milk income, Indrapura would register at the top in the entire district. Right from the start, its model was Amul but now that is not the case. Now there is a triumphant glee that Amul has declined and they, the Dudhsagar villages, have forged ahead. Currently, its milk cooperative membership is about 400. Out of this, the Chaudhuries constitute 230 and they have made the milk miracle possible. Then there are the BCs and SCs, and they too are a part of this achievement. The greatness of the Indrapura milk cooperative is that out of 45 landless people in the village, 21 have been inducted into its milk cooperative as members. There are 131 marginal farmers, 51 small farmers, and 31 large farmers.

The development of the highly successful milk cooperative movement in the district of Mehsana has thus served its economy in a variety of ways. Apart from achieving the top ranking among the milk cooperatives of India, Dudhsagar has vitally strengthened the agricultural economy of the district. For one thing, the income from milk is a year round income for farmers, unlike agricultural crops which are seasonal. Consequently, for the farmer, income from milk has acted as a much needed cushion in periods of low cash flow from agricultural crops. Farmers of the district also remember the period of indebtedness, which they suffered from in between crops. Now many of their transactions are carried out on cash basis. The availability of cash has also helped farmers become bolder in their experiments. They can employ more laborers and get more water by having bore wells, if their tracts of land can sustain such expenditure. Otherwise, they get into cooperative or joint arrangements for water with their neighbors or relatives.

Simultaneously, an increasing number of farmers graduate to the status of urban dwellers by undertaking commercial ventures in burgeoning towns of the district such as Vijapur, Patan, Harij, Kheralu, Kadi, etc. Until around the middle of the 1980s, they had confined themselves to opening of shops in urban centers. Since then, they, like Kheda Patidars, have also moved to small-scale industries in big towns such as Kadi, Mehsana, etc. The milk money, which hitherto had gone into agriculture, has now started to be used for setting up of small industrial units in the district.

The liquidity generated by milk, as stated earlier, initially helped the milk producers push their district into a dairy-agriculture-dairy cycle. More money meant greater capacity for water, which in turn gave rise to more greenery, which could then sustain more animals, and so forth. In the subsequent phase, that liquidity helped build financial support for commercial and real estate development in the smaller towns of the district. But from the mid-1970s onwards, so many smaller industrial units came up by way of the need to support the rapidly developing transport sector, foundries, and parts needed for rapidly industrializing small towns near the city of Ahmedabad. Moreover, gas, oil, ceramic, and pharmaceutical industries in the district, which have made great strides in the last decade, also depend on various machine parts, which the local manufactures can supply. So Mehsana district now has its development taking place at two ends: from the rural communities to small towns with the help of milk economy, or what may be termed "base up"; and in smaller towns from the rapidly extending major industries from larger cities, or "top down." The result: the district and the city of Mehsana are literally exploding with development possibilities.

Once you move away from the two great milk cooperatives of India, namely, Amul and Dudhsagar (both of them the outgrowths of Indian national movement), you come across a variety of cooperatives, which were burdened by additional problems, both human and physical.

IV. Overcoming Environmental Limitations

Sabar, in Gujarat, is a cooperative with environmental limitations. Located in a small town called Himmatnagar, in the district of Sabarkantha (adjacent to Mehsana district), Sabar dairy had to face problems that were unprecedented. While there were flourishing pockets of milk production in some of its subdistricts, the rest of the district did not even have a preceding agricultural development on which dairying depended. Soon after India's independence, money started pouring into the district for buying its land, which had a good many agricultural possibilities. However, those who bought land, mostly Patidars from other areas, stayed away from its villages and settled on their own farms. They did not feel secure in the villages, as they were from outside. The district also had its own component of Chaudhuries who displayed keenness for dairy development. Then there were Kshatriyas and lower castes, who had virtually no experience of dairying. What proved most difficult for the builders of cooperatives in the district was how to set up institutions that could be operated by the farmers themselves. It therefore needed more experienced farmers to set up cooperative institutions and run them. Sabar Dairy, for this purpose, approached the farmers of a subdistrict called Prantij, with a large Patidar population who, so far, had sent milk to the city of Ahmedabad with the help of milk traders. The Prantij Patidars responded favorably and set up milk cooperative institutions in their subdistrict, which then became a model for other subdistricts to emulate. Ironically, in order to reach out to the poor, Sabar dairy had to take the help of rich Patidars to set up a model for the poor to follow. The Sabar experience thus consisted of approaching the prosperous farmers to build milk cooperatives first so that the less prosperous may imitate them in the adjoining areas. In less than two decades, after the setting up of Sabar dairy, the district started getting a steady income from the sale of milk.

In the mid 1980s Sabar dairy started procuring 350,000 litres of milk per day. Fifteen years later, when we revisited it, the amount of milk collected had doubled to about 700,000 litres a day. In fact, it was as much as that of Amul's procurement during the same period. Despite a shaky start, and the human and natural disadvantages, Sabar had moved into the category of viable cooperatives. In 1999 it ploughed into the district's economy a sum of Rs.400 crores (U.S.$ 82.47m).

The importance attached to Prantij, as a model, gradually disappeared. The Chaudhuries of the district, who had employed a lot of farm hands, mostly from tribal communities, had now begun to pass on their know-how about dairying to them. That, in turn, helped a number of tribal villages increase their income from milk.

In the year 2000, the Chaudhury villages of the district looked extraordinarily prosperous. Drought conditions had forced them to put their money into dairying. This increased their income from milk still further. Some of them regretted that they had to withdraw from agriculture but considering their income, they were not unhappy with the change.

This was also true, to a great extent, of tribal villages. They too had switched their investment increasingly into dairying. In a tribal subdistrict called Khedbrahamma, a number of tribals had benefited by working in the cowsheds of the Chaudhuries. Like the Chaudhuries, the tribals were able to get a steady income from dairying during the difficult period of drought. So dairying had come to them as a great blessing. One could switch one's resources and sit out the famine. In those lean years, the membership of milk cooperatives went up and so did their milk collection.

As in Mehsana district, Sabar district too had its mega milk villages, with milk income ranging from Rs.1.7 crores (U.S. $377,777) to Rs.4 crores (U.S.$888,888). But there were few such villages. Despite severe drought in the district, the youthful mana-gerial team of Sabar had succeeded in getting national productivity awards. Its team, led by Dr. Mayur Vyas, managing director, had succeeded in getting the coveted quality certification known as "ISO 9002." That was the first in cooperative dairying. After that, word went out that others should also strive for the certification.

Sabar also claimed that its success in milk cooperatives had helped make the district highly conscious of cooperatives as an alternative route to take for its social and economic development. Suddenly the district had emerged as a center of cooperatives of all kinds. By 1999 it had a large number of people who had joined 29 different cooperatives operating in just one district.[2] Sabar, a rela-tively less known dairy cooperative, had thus succeeded in stimulating intense competition among cooperatives of Gujarat.

Close on the heels of Sabar there was yet another dairy, called Banas, in the adjoining district, which also had registered phenom-enal growth. Like Sabar, Banas had to contend with limitations of human and natural resources. Apart from poor agricultural condi-tions, Banas district was known for its general backwardness. It had even neglected one of its finest animal resources, namely, the *Kanjrej cow.*

Soon after its inception, Banas started attracting agriculturists who could not survive in the near-desert conditions and the repeated failure of rainfall. They, therefore, switched to dairying. Simultaneously, a recession in the diamond polishing industry in the district also pushed a number of investors into dairying. Banas dairy, therefore, had to continually expand its processing plant to be able to handle the growing amount of milk. Its dairy plant also became the largest industrial unit in the district, which employed 1,200 workers.

Since dairying had become some kind of a refuge industry for the people of this drought prone district, the funds generated by the sale of milk was ploughed back into dairying itself. With the result, Banas was dubbed the fastest growing milk cooperative of Gujarat. Even people in Dudhsagar maintained that one day Banas would overtake it in milk production. In 1996 it received a national award for productivity and was dubbed "an oasis in the desert" (Banas Dairy n.d.).

By 1997-1998, Banas Dairy, located in a lesser-known district of India, with all its environmental limitations, had ploughed back into the district's economy a substantial sum of money. Equally impressive was the background of its members. Nearly sixty percent of its membership consisted of the landless, and marginal and small farmers. (Cited from a note prepared by Banas Dairy staff.)

Banas thus provides us with another example of how a district could rise despite several limitations. The remarkable thing about it was that once cooperative institutions were put in place, and their members were convinced that those institutions were working for them, the income of milk producers rose faster than the organizers could handle. In 1997-1998, Banas procured 750,000 litres of milk. Then in 1998-1999 it jumped to 848,000 litres, coming close to the premier dairies with one million litres in flush season. But there were fluctuations in its total procurement as every other year severe drought conditions unsettled a number of milk producers and forced them and their cattle to migrate to areas where there was water.

By the 1980s the villagers had learned how to operate milk cooperatives based on the "Anand Pattern" and also to extract maxi-mum benefit out of the various services that it provided. Then came the price stimulus. The surplus milk in Gujarat could now reach different parts of India as a result of an emerging milk grid and an adequate network of transport facilities to support it. In the late 1990s, Banas was once again looking for yet another milk processing unit, as its existing facilities could not handle what it procured.

As stated earlier, while nature had not favored the district with good environmental conditions, as it borders on the deserts of North-west India, it did bless it with great animals, which, alas, were not cared for properly. *Kankarej* cows, which had been the pride of this region, were neglected for years. So was a variety called *gir*. The milk producing community of Banas did not look after its indigenous cattle wealth like the people of Mehsana. To that, there was one exception. The local bull, *Banni*, which in the past was considered to be a great animal, was making a comeback. In the meanwhile, the local cows were almost indiscriminately crossed with the semen of foreign breeds. Banas had yet to develop an infrastructure of veterinary research and show results that could convince the milk-producing community to switch to other animals.

Banas had spent much of its time consolidating itself as a milk union. Such a situation did not allow it to do long term planning either to improve its animals or to reach out to the poorest in the district. In a village that had a population of tribal, and Kshatriyas, locally known as *garasias*, the latter, as a result of the failure of agriculture, had increasingly turned to bootlegging and had also involved tribal youths in their illicit trade. Banas had yet to help tribal youths out with dairying, which after bootlegging seemed much less attractive.

V. Taking the Cooperatives to the Tribals

This brings us to some of the milk unions of Gujarat, which made a superhuman effort to bring into the cooperatives some of the most neglected people of India, namely, the *adivasis* or tribals. Both Sumul in Surat and Vasudhara in Valsad did just that. In their incredible enterprise, the social activists of all shades operating in their respective districts assisted them.

It is often claimed that the district of Surat has been the main center of cooperative thinking in India since Mahatma Gandhi launched Bardoli *sataygraha* in 1928. To Gandhi, cooperatives seemed to be an alternative to colonial policy trying to emasculate indigenous economic activity. And the district of Surat was one of the earliest to give expression to it. Its cooperative workers claimed that: "Surat District has been a pioneer in India in channeling trade in Cotton and Milk through co-operatives." (A brief note about Sumul Dairy, prepared by the staff of Sumul Dairy, prior to our interview in 1999.) The cooperative veterans of Surat were therefore not at all happy about Kheda district stealing a march over them when it went out to establish Amul Dairy in 1946.

The district of Surat, however, had one problem and that is it wanted to cooperatize, simultaneously, many areas of economic activity and therefore could not come up with a cogent proposal for building its own milk industry. Nevertheless, there were two distinct advantages coming out of Surat's cooperative heritage, namely, intense pragmatism and a deep commitment to social activism. The former found expression in building textile, cotton, fruits, and vegetable cooperatives, and the latter assisted in inducting the tribals of the district into the cooperative dairy network. In building milk cooperatives in tribal villages, as we shall see in this and the next chapter, Sumul, and later on Vasudhara of Valsad, displayed a rare degree of social idealism that has continued to this day. They thus combined the economic development of the district with the human development of the tribals within cooperative institutions.

Tribals constitute nearly fifty percent of Surat district's population. For Sumul dairy, it was easy to build milk cooperatives in rural communities, inhabited by Patidars and Desais, the two economically prosperous castes with good education and who lived on irrigated land. But it required a lot of social idealism and painstaking work to build milk cooperatives in tribal villages. The tribals did not have milch animals worth the name. Nor did they have any experience of managing institutions like milk cooperatives. It involved collecting milk, testing it for fat content, measuring it, pouring it into milk cans to keep time with the transport people, maintaining records of individual pourers, giving them cash regularly after every two weeks, and then arranging for veterinary services, etc. Over a period of nearly twenty years, Sumul achieved this gigantic task and established milk cooperatives in most of the tribal villages. For that purpose, it was fortunate to have the services of its senior veterinarian, Dr. H.A. Ghasia, and his assistant Dr. Dilip Shah who, together, built most of those cooperatives. At times it was difficult to tell whether they were veterinarians or social activists. In the winter of 1999-2000, the organizers of Sumul told us that it collected nearly 80 percent of its total milk requirements from tribal villages. Sumul's highly dedicated staff had thus brought about a double revolution: it inducted India's most poor and neglected people into mainstream dairying, and it also provided them with an income which then changed their economic and social life. As Sumul's note puts it: "out of its total membership of 198,500; 85 percent of them [are] tribals, who contribute 80 percent of the total annual milk procured by Sumul. Sumul is a pioneer organization which has brought in its fold such a number of tribals" (Sumul Dairy 1999).

Sumul Dairy is located in Gujrat's second largest city, Surat, which, incidentally, has an insatiable demand for pasteurized milk. It therefore had the most favorable market condition for milk than any other cooperative of India with the exception of Gokul in Kolhapur, which had linked itself to the city of Mumbai. Sumul was therefore able to give highly attractive prices for milk to its producers. That was the reason why more and more farmers wanted to get into dairying. Returns from milk were not only good; they were also steady because of the demand for milk all year round. Apart from an assured market for the producers all year round, Sumul's staff maintained a regular contact with its rural communities. Moreover, the presence of a large number of social activists –who were influenced by leaders such as Jayprakash Narayan and Jugatram Dave, who themselves were some kind of militant Gandhians—also helped. They vigorously supported cooperatives of all kinds.

In the 1970s, Sumul used to collect 17,000 litres of milk per day from its villages. Thirty years later that had gone up to 550,000 litres per day, more than thirty-two times. The tribals joined milk cooperatives in a big way because they could not get much out of the poor quality of their land. With money from milk, they started improving their land. In 2000, Sumul dairy staff told us that nearly 40 percent of district's sugarcane crop came from adivasi villages. Rural Surat, despite its huge adivasi population, had now snowballed into a rapidly developing rural economy where a dairying-agriculture-dairying expanding cycle, like Mehsana's, may be emerging. Apart from increased purchase of appliances, gold, jewelry, and expenses on wedding, there is quite a lot of money left in those communities awaiting further investment. This is one reason why there is an explosion of thrift and credit groups across rural Gujarat, and much more in districts where their milk economies have done well. They now buy a good percentage of appliances manufactured in India. For the first time in recent history, rural Gujarat has money to spare. And there is a strong belief across its villages that now its money will start earning money and there will be an abundance of prosperity.

Such then was the mood following the entry of the tribals into the mainstream economy. The *adivasis* of Surat have now emerged as the new agriculturists of the district with one difference; their principal source of income is from dairying, which puts them on a more secure footing than those who entirely depend on agriculture. Shopkeepers in their villages now have a brisk business as compared to earlier years when they used to while away their time watching traffic. There is also a decline in the number of money-lenders and a corresponding rise in banks in those villages.

In the past, the prosperity of five major subdistricts, namely,

Olpad, Choryasi, Kamrej, Pulsana, and Bardoli, had been due to the availability of water. The Desais and Patidars, the two upper castes of the region, were the main beneficiaries of the prosperity. But the subdisticts, with heavy concentrations of tribal population such as Mangrol, Mandavi, Vyara, Songarh, Nizar, and Uchhal, did not do so well. Even their attempts to start milk cooperatives were discouraged because the upper castes depended on cheap agricultural labor from the tribals. Finally, when the *adivasis* did succeed in having those institutions, both the Patidars and Desais joined them. The transition within the cooperatives was therefore relatively smooth.

Bolder than the Surat venture was the Vasudhara cooperative development in the adjoining district of Valsad. Like Surat, it too has the same proportion of its population consisting of tribals. When Vasudhara started building cooperatives in tribal villages, it put women in charge of them. Tribal women now run more than 60 percent of the cooperatives in the district. Early on the top organizers of Vasudhara came to the conclusion that they should extend dairying facilities to the tribals, particularly to their women. The result was that they were able to bring into the workforce a hitherto untapped resource, namely, women. The induction of tribal women into milk cooperatives resulted in an inordinate rise in milk production. So much so that in 1993-1994 and 1995-1996, Valsad was able to win national productivity awards and thereby was able to attract the attention of the premier milk cooperatives of India. The implications of bringing in women are far-reaching. Women are exposed to the workings of an economic institution and also to the ideas and suggestions of a number of specialists, including the veterinarians and dairymen. After such exposure and experience, women are no longer confined to their domestic chores and children, but are connected to the dairy organization, its resources, personnel, skills, and its ever-expanding infrastructure and opportunities. And if they are lucky to have social activists in the region interested in their development, then there is the possibility of discussing education, health, and career prospects for their children.

Some of the women told us how they used to do backbreaking

majoori (physical labor) on construction sites. Now they do not have to do that. Also, their children can spend more time in school. With income from dairying not only had they found an escape route from poverty, but they also found the means to more education for their children and their development in general.

One of the immediate effects of tribal women's involvement in cooperative dairying, and their learning more about money, was that they were now more responsive to the attempts of social activists to involve them in micro saving and lending groups. In less than three years, the tribal women, right across the district, were buzzing with the talk of how much they could save and the good returns that could be acquired.

While the social composition of the district of Valsad presented one profile, namely, the preponderance of adivasis as milk producers, its geographical location and business opportunities presented another, and that is the urban markets of the city of Mumbai and Nagpur, Vasudhara, therefore, had to develop a dual personality to be able to serve the underclass of the district along with the affluent and educated clients of the two urban centres. Vasudhara's annual report for the year 2003 bore testimony to that. It profusely thanked its social activist staff, who worked assiduously in its remote adivasi villages, and also its technocrats, manufacturing engineers and marketing experts who, together helped it to market value-added milk products with the best returns possible.

VI. Benefiting from Urban Linkages

One of the reasons why the milk cooperatives could offer better returns to their grassroots members was because of how the cooperatives were organized and governed. In that respect, the Anand Pattern cooperatives, which were largely managed by elected representatives of milk producers, had a good record. As opposed to the government-run cooperatives or organizations, with all their delays and corruption, the Anand Pattern cooperatives had an impressive record of probity and result-oriented professional management.

Politicians, bureaucrats, and traders, naturally, did not favor such cooperatives. Moreover, rarely was a government-managed cooperative able to make a transition to a self-managed Anand Pattern cooperative. One of the rare ones able to do so was the Gokul Dairy in the city of Kolapur, and the results were stunning.

Established in 1963, Gokul Dairy in Mahrastra state was run like a government department. Despite good animals and plenty of water, it was not doing as well as some of the dairies in the neighboring state of Gujarat. Consequently in 1978, Gokul took the bold step of opting for an Aanad Pattern cooperative. For such a transition, it received the support of social activists and the socially concerned retired, and repentant, bureaucrats of the region. But that was not the end of its problems. The district of Kolhapur was well known for its sugarcane crop, and the big landowners ran the sugar cooperatives. They did not always believe in transparency and regular elections. As opposed to that, the Anand Pattern cooperatives held their elections regularly. Everything that the latter did was open to public scrutiny. Hence, the two sets of cooperative norms, in sugar and milk cooperatives, came into conflict.

The hard work of Gokul's organizers and social activists, good veterinary services and regular cash payments, and elimination of the middleman's cut resulted in a huge increase in milk productivity and procurement. In 1967, when Gokul emerged from the clutches of a government department, its procurement was barely 29,000 litres. In 1985 it jumped to 300,000 litres and in 1998 it soared to 550,000 litres.

By 1999, Gokul had started ploughing back large sums of money into the district's grassroots economy on a regular basis. It also gave employment to nearly 1,500 people, and stimulated the transport and road building industry. But Gokul did not want to stop there. Given its proximity to Mumbai's huge market, it wanted to get the best price for its producers. Consequently, given the freedom to act as a self-governing organization, it began getting the maximum advantage of its urban linkages with the city of Mumbai.

While Kolhapur succeeded in getting the maximum benefit for its milk producers because of its linkages with urban markets, those in Tamil Nadu, and to some extent Andhra Pradesh in the south, did not. This time the problem was not from the interfering bureaucrats but the elected politicians. In Tamil Nadu, the milk unions in the districts of Erode, Salem, and North Arcott were not allowed to charge the consumers in the city of Chennai what was reasonable to charge in other cities of India. The politicians in Tamil Nadu depressed the prices in order to please the urban voters. They did not allow market mechanisms to determine the price of milk as was done in Gujarat, Maharastra, and elsewhere. The result was many milk producers, most of them marginal farmers and the landless, went out of business. The same was true in the case of *Ponlait* in the Union Territory of Pondicherry. It could not determine its own price without government interference.

In Andhra Pradesh, the elected politicians interfered with cooperative dairy in yet another fashion, forcing them to collect milk for private dairies. There was agitation against such practice, largely spearheaded by women.

In the state of Karnataka, despite interference by elected politicians its district cooperatives, because of the urban linkages, have done fairly well. Both Bangalore and Kolar milk unions ploughed back a good sum of money in the economies of their respective districts. While Bangalore milk union concentrated on the market in the city itself, Kolar got the benefit of marketing milk in the equally prosperous peri-urban areas of the metropolis. In both those districts, marginal farmers and landless had also benefited enormously by becoming members of village milk cooperatives.

VII.   Milk Cooperatives with Difficult Beginnings

It is not always easy to reach out to the poor in developing countries. Any effort, even with a clear grasp of the complexity of local situation, takes much longer to produce results. Such was the case in a few major states of India. Elected politicians with their base of support in caste groups, together with corrupt bureaucrats, saw to it that nothing was done that would undermine their hold on political power or eliminate their sources of illicit income.

The two states in question are Bihar and Uttar Pradesh (UP) in India. Historically speaking, they have been the seat of India's classical civilization and learning, a source of its major religions such as Hinduism, Buddhism, Sikhism, and the Indian versions of Islam. They were also some of the best-administered states during the colonial rule. They incubated and then launched, along with other states, the Indian national movement for independence. UP, in particular, also gave to the country most of its prime ministers. But after independence, their consistent decline earned them the humiliating status of *bimaru* (sick) states where almost nothing worked. The rest of India blamed them for spoiling the nation's statistics of illiteracy, poverty, births and deaths, lawlessness and, in short, everything that gave the country a bad name. Since Bihar was the poorer of the two, the cooperative movement tried to concentrate its efforts there. A lot of patience was required to install its infrastructure and train the regional personnel. The NDDB, which took milk cooperatives to Bihar, even gave the assurance that it would bear all the losses while the state of Bihar could keep the profits, if there were any.

Before the NDDB got into the act, the district of Patna, in Bihar, set up a cattle feed plant and a cooperative dairy in 1977 and 1978, respectively. Because of the improper implementation of the plans, both failed. In 1979, the then chief minister asked the NDDB to take over the project. In 1981, floods, followed by disease, ravaged Bihar. This put an additional responsibility on the NDDB team to provide fodder and medicines. Such a service, rare in Bihar, won the hearts and minds of milk producers. The cooperative personnel not only saved the animals from disease but also administered, with the help of local doctors, vaccinations to 35,000 children.

From this difficult beginning the cooperative movement learned an important lesson: it is necessary to do many other things for the needy before introducing them to dairying proper. And there again, if you can bring in women to look after not only the cowsheds, which they routinely do, but also to run the village-level cooperative organization itself, they would then insulate the institution from outside political influence. And this is what the NDDB did in Bihar wherever possible. Suddenly, the picture changed. Cooperatives run by women earned audit ratings of A+ because they were well managed. They also began pouring large sums of money into the villages. The local as well as national newspapers hailed their achievement as a "success story." In a state where there were few success stories, the achievement of a milk cooperative dairy stood out as a shining example of what *can* be done if one went about things the right way. When the milk producers were polled for the benefits that they had received through the milk cooperatives, 94 percent stated that it had improved their standard of living. It was remarkable that 66 percent of the membership of these cooperatives came from backward castes, and 18 percent were women.

After teething troubles, the state of Bihar came to have milk unions of its own which were known as Vaishal-Patliputra, Barauni, Samastipur, Mithila, Tirhut, and Shahbad. Together these unions ploughed back into the villages a sum of Rs.40 crore (US$8.88m) per year. Their success was largely due to the cooperation which they received from Bihar's politically dominant agriculturist caste, namely, the Yadavs.

Let us now consider another example of the tortuous beginnings (as a result of bureaucratic delays) of the cooperative movement in an equally poor state, Rajasthan. Apart from the usual problems connected with the development of milk cooperatives in an economically backward state, Rajasthan presented a fiercely independent view on the nature of milk cooperatives. Relatively young and inexperienced bureaucrats insisted that Rajasthan was not Gujarat, and therefore the Anand Pattern of milk cooperative was not suitable. It should have what they called the "Rajasthan Pattern" of milk cooperatives. In making such a case, they had not consulted many people.

From the perspective of the bureaucrats, Rajasthan had the longest surviving feudal past and, as a result, was not a suitable place for an Anand-type, farmer-owned and operated cooperative. They believed that in the running of cooperatives, there should be a provision for the supervisory role of bureaucrats to oversee what was occurring. In effect, it was a vote of "no confidence" in their own people, belittling their ability to learn from their own mistakes in a democratic situation. This tussle, between the NDDB and Rajasthan bureaucracy, went on for quite sometime. The bureaucrats also succeeded in getting funds to try out their own version of cooperatives. Thus, too much time was wasted without helping the poor in any way. Finally, the bureaucrats were told by politicians not to stand in the way of the widely accepted Anand Pattern cooperatives. Reluctantly, they agreed.

By 1997, there were 16 milk unions in Rajasthan, which covered 27 of its districts. In nine years, the NDDB staff was able to establish milk unions in Jaipur, Bhilwada, Ajmer, Ganganagar, Alwar, Bikaner, Bharatpur, Pali, Sirohi, Udaipur, Banaswada, Churu, Jodhpur, Sikar, Tonk-Sawaimadhopur, and Kota. Their performance was also ranked in that order. Most of these unions were economically viable and did not depend on the state to help them financially. These district unions, however, had to go a long way towards improving the quality of their animals. One of their significant achievements, as we shall see later on, was to bring women into milk cooperatives and, in some cases, put them in charge despite opposition.

There was, however, a curious governmental presence in all the things that Rajasthan did, including the starting of milk cooperatives. The chastened bureaucrats finally set up cooperatives to help the poor as well as women. But in that state you could never get away from government. Consequently, in a number of important positions in various unions, the government of the day insisted on appointing civil servants to senior positions, and to that extent, the application of Anand Pattern of cooperatives was subverted. As opposed to Gujarat, where dairy movement tried to remain as independent of government as possible, in Rajasthan, from day one, the hand of government was all-pervasive.

The working of participatory institutions of milk cooperatives, especially at the grassroots level, was facilitated by the leadership provided by its politically dominant agriculturist caste, namely, the Jats. The Jats were also administrative functionaries at various levels of state bureaucracy. Together, they often cut across the division between politics and administration.

Despite the educational and economic backwardness, the state of Rajasthan is blessed with a large number of urban NGOs operating in its rural communities. They too have given a helping hand in operating participatory institutions of milk cooperatives. Quite often they have gone beyond it in strengthening the state's accountability movement by forcing the top administrators to explain development expense in specific rural communities when in fact there is hardly any evidence of it.

Before we move on to some general observations, it might be appropriate here to provide a comparative picture of the earnings of various milk unions that we examined in different parts of India. Their comparative earnings from the sale of milk was as follows:

Statement indicating Total Kg Fat received and the Cost per KG FAT

Name of the Union	Cost Per KG FAT	Total KG FAT Received	Amount passed on to Producers (Rs. in Millions)	U.S.$ in Millions
1. Sumul	207.92	12652073	2630.619018	58.4582
2. Valsad	185.15	3890192	720.2690488	16.006
3. Amul	175.36	15307053	2684.244814	59.6499
4. Banas	180	17315957	3116.87226	69.2638
5. Mehsana	184.6	28468540	5255.292484	116.784
6. Sabar	185	16226862	3001.96947	66.7104
7. Bangalore	205.62	8380662	1723.23172	38.294
8. Kolapur	195.63	11728983	2294.540944	50.9898

Source: This chart was provided by the National Dairy Development Board .

VIII. Some General Observations

Context-Effective Measures

India did not wait for a high economic tide to lift some of its poor out of poverty, rather, it devised context-effective measures to tackle part of this massive problem. While the planners and politicians of independent India put their faith in planned economy and bureaucracy to reduce poverty, the milk cooperative movement, together with its emerging professional class and social activists, explored alternative forms of remedial action; and in that they had a huge success. As stated earlier, by the year 2000 the milk cooperative movement had touched the lives of more than 60 million people and, given its growth rate of more than 7 to 10 percent per annum, it was likely to touch many more in the years to come. It had, in effect, created its own "tide," which will remain a significant player in poverty-reduction programs in the future.

Combination of Available Resources

A distinguished British political scientist, W.H. Morris-Jones, had once remarked that India is a country where "centuries co-exist." In rural India, where the bulk of the population lives, most people go about their social and economic life in their traditional ways, while in urban India there are developments in the fields of manufacturing, management, science, and information technology that are world class and in world-wide demand. Very few sectors of the Indian economy have been able to combine these two worlds, but the cooperative dairies have, and with great effect. While the milk producers go about their business in their cowsheds in their traditional fashion, the veterinarians and their experiments are continually improving the cattle breeds. Similarly, the veterinarians and their associates have also been able to extend animal health service and artificial insemination to grassroots communities.

Furthermore, those communities are now aware of the new modes of transporting, processing, packaging, and marketing of milk and milk products. The latest advancement to arrive in those rural communities is the computer, the presence of which had stunned President Clinton when he visited a village called Nyala in Rajasthan in 1999.

These grassroots cooperatives have not compelled milk producers to suddenly change their ways. That would not have worked. Rather, they have exposed them to modern ways of doing things right in their own backyard and, further, have waited for them to adapt to the new ways. Meanwhile, as the milk is collected and transported to processing plants, state of the art technology and the most modern methods of quality control are adopted and this enables the cooperatives to compete in the indigenous and world markets. Such a judicious approach has paid great dividends.

An Organization of the Neglected

What began as an organization of milk producers, regardless of their background, eventually became an institution of small farmers, the landless, and the socially disadvantaged. The initial aim of cooperatives was to eliminate the profit of the middlemen; provide professional management, services, and market expertise; and give maximum benefit to milk producers. But in due course, the cooperatives became involved in the question of how to help induct more and more of the economically weaker segments of rural society. For this they had to persuade district and state governments to give relatively resourceless people loans and subsidies, enabling them to become "milk producers," and enter the cooperatives.

The confidence of the milk cooperatives in the economically weaker segments of rural society was not misplaced. The OBCs, in particular, turned some of the villages into mega milk communities, generating enough surplus to experiment with cash crop or commercial and industrial ventures. What the cooperatives did, in effect, was to give them facilities to fulfill their economic potentials as milk producers and then set them on course to explore new opportunities on their own. A continent-sized society and economy, with its own continuing historical and social problems, needed many more facilities and opportunities for its individuals to regenerate their own dynamism and then tackle bigger, continent-size problems. These cooperatives in their modest way did precisely that. They took a section of the poor off the list of the destitute so that the state institutions, with their meager resources, could reach those that the cooperatives could not. The cooperatives thus shared the public burden without fanfare or political payoff. Their only reward, as reflected in the eyes and faces of those social activists who built and helped operate grassroots institutions, was one of deep personal satisfaction. It is to their unique contribution that we now turn.

Chapter 2

Involving the Socially Concerned to Fight Poverty

T he dairy revolution, which targeted the poor, would not have been possible without the participation of social activists. They came from a variety of backgrounds and brought with them various skills and a deep understanding of the nature of poverty and social disadvantage in rural India. Some of them mobilized the poor from ground zero, whereas others worked with them in cooperative institutions and prepared them to take on the responsibility of self-management. Even dairy technologists, veterinarians, and technical people in general took on the role of social activist in order to be more effective. Without such a pool of social activists, such a gigantic cooperative undertaking in such a large country, with a backlog of social and economic problems, would not have been possible.

Despite apparent similarities among the cooperatives, there were differences in their emphasis on what they could do once their basic participatory structures were put in place. The very emergence of a new cooperative community, across the traditional social divide, was enough to give rise to the hope that it could do more. Moreover, improvements in their economic condition encouraged the community of milk producers to experiment, to explore avenues for further progress along with dairying and, if necessary, without it. They viewed dairying as an initial phase in their social and economic development with a mind to move on to something else. In this chapter, we shall explore these and other related issues.

This chapter is divided into the following subsections: (I) Different Kinds of Milk Cooperatives; (II) Offshoots of the Indian National Movement; (III) Targeting the Poor and Neglected; (IV) From

Governmentalism to Cooperatism; (V) Poverty and the Role of Social Activists; and (VI) Some General Observations.

I. Different Kinds of Milk Cooperatives

The various cooperatives in India had different beginnings and these beginnings often determined their subsequent direction, despite the strong influence of the Anand Pattern cooperative. In fact, the demand for the Anand Pattern often restricted itself to the representative character of grassroots and district level institutions, with enough freedom to market their own products. In actual practice, however, different cooperatives shaped themselves differently as a result of their social and economic background, leadership, and the work done by social activists. Some of the cooperatives went well beyond what was prescribed by Anand Pattern, whereas others barely met its requirements. Given the enormous diversity in India, and the differing developmental dynamics of its regions, this was something to be expected. The NDDB provided the institutional infrastructure and trained personnel, and offered marketing facilities and initial funding. The regional leaders and social activists enrolled members, prepared them for new programs and policies, and attended to the day-to-day operations of the institutions. Broadly speaking, these cooperatives fell under the following five categories.

Grassroots-Initiated Cooperatives

These cooperatives produced their own grassroots leadership, prior to the arrival of an NDDB appointed spearhead team. In fact, such teams often came in response to their demand. The grassroots cooperatives opted for an Anand Pattern type participatory cooperative without reservation. Sometimes it even approached the NDDB to expedite the formal paperwork so that they could get down to business. Such cooperatives also had a strong component of voluntary activity and cooperative initiative, which then helped them retain their deeply prized participatory character, questioning culture, and demand for accountability. They continually explored new cooperative horizons for their members and made efforts to bring the economically weakest segments of rural society into the milk producing community. They also pressured their district or union level organizations to go into other areas of community needs such as loans and subsidies, health, educational programs, and so on.

Groundwork-Based Cooperatives

These cooperatives were created after district or state level political leaders and social workers had done the initial groundwork. That was particularly true of the early years of the milk cooperative movement when there was very little understanding of what they were all about. But as more and more milk cooperatives came into existence, and the results of their operations were there for the neighboring regions to examine, there was correspondingly less justification to go to milk producers and ask them to join such institutions. Such a need, however, continued in areas inhabited by economically weaker segments or in remote regions that were cut off from mainstream economic life.

Once those regions or segments of rural society obtained the operative knowledge, and received the accompanying economic benefits, they developed their own potential and dynamics and even overtook, in the quality of their operations, some of those cooperative institutions that had the benefit of a grassroots leadership.

Cooperatives that Required Constant Supervision

Such cooperatives went through many ups and downs. Quite often dissension in their leadership resulted in the need for close supervision. Sometimes their weaknesses were also the result of interference by meddlesome bureaucrats and/or wily state politicians. Some of these cooperatives, though not all, eventually graduated from "sick" status to thriving, self-governing institutions.

Cooperatives Run by Government Departments

In those states of India where the grassroots movement was weak, the departments of agriculture established milk cooperatives and exercised rigid control over them. Their rationale always was that cooperatives were complex institutions and therefore required the specialized knowledge of administration, which only IAS (Indian Administrative Service) level bureaucrats could provide. In other states, the argument was that politicians might get into those cooperatives and use them for their selfish purposes and, therefore, there existed a need for senior bureaucrats to manage the cooperatives.

The case that bureaucrats made against self-governing cooperatives was not always convincing. This is because they, the bureaucrats, were often negative and even obstructionist in their approach, which almost always stifled the grassroots initiatives. Rarely did they bother to understand, or even consider, the need for a different kind of administration for cooperatives. Equally questionable was their claim that they were less corrupt than the politicians. Quite often, the bureaucrats were in league with the politicians.

The practice of stifling grassroots initiatives had a lasting consequence. Cooperatives, which came through such a route, took longer to realize that within the limits of cooperative bylaws, they were the masters of their own economic destiny. This meant that they could learn about, and modify, the operations of their institutions democratically, more efficiently, and also seek accountability from their decision makers and policy implementers as they went along.

Continual Political Interference in Cooperatives

Even within this broad classification, one can make a distinction between grassroots cooperatives, which succeeded in challenging the interference by state governments, politicians, and bureaucrats, and those that did not. Here, again, the grassroots cooperatives of

Gujarat demonstrated greater resistance and attempted to use the courts to fight outside interference. Since politicians are continually seeking control over cooperatives, even when the courts chastise them, they do not give up their efforts; they keep trying. Within Gujarat, there are the examples of Amul and Banas, which dragged the politicians to court and won partial or full victory against interference. The cooperatives could not afford to lower their guard.

While the grassroots milk cooperatives of Gujarat succeeded in keeping the politicians at a distance, as far as milk prices were concerned, those in Tamil Nadu, as we saw in Chapter 1, were not so fortunate. There, the politicians interfered with the price structure so as to ensure votes for themselves in urban constituencies. On other occasions, in order to get credit for themselves, they allowed milk cooperatives to function with minimum interference. This was also true of Bihar. Even its controversial politicians allowed milk cooperatives to function with minimum interference and took credit for their success.

II. Offshoots of the Indian National Movement

The pre- and post-independence periods in India have left behind two contrasting legacies. The former left behind a living tradition of social activism and a healthy skepticism of government. And the latter, until around 1990s, put an inordinate faith in government initiatives and public control. The cooperative dairy movement received a great deal of support from social activists and obstruction, spread over half a century, from bureaucrats. The bureaucrats, in particular, nurtured by Nehru socialism, also became a bastion of bureaucratic negativism and corruption. Even when the cooperative movement combined social activism with technocratic and managerial skills, and produced great results, it could not make itself immune to bureaucratic interference and subversion; that danger persisted. In politics, as in administration, one of the self-evident truths is that you can never, once and for all, tell either a politician or a bureaucrat to go away and to not interfere in areas where they have no legitimate claim. No amount of snubbing, legal or political, is effective enough. So, one way to defend cooperatives is to have adequate legislation that can give them legal protection. But legislation in itself will not obviate the need for constant vigilance on the part of social activists who have a hand in running these grassroots institutions.

The more the cooperative movement succeeded in India, the greater was its realization of what more was needed. Dr. Kurien aptly expresses this: "We need genuine cooperatives, owned and controlled by their members and managed by real professionals. To achieve this we need new cooperative laws, laws that are enabling not prescriptive; laws that leave to the members the decisions that affect the resources they produce;...laws that do not allow political interest to hijack a business that is serving people regardless of language, religion, caste or political affiliation" (Kurien 1996:xiv-xv).

The major milk cooperatives of India emerged precisely in regions where they could combine the cooperative movement with the tradition of social activism. This gave them an effective starting point as well as operational standards, practices, a questioning attitude, and direct or indirect emphasis on grassroots participation. Along with this, the cooperatives were able to bring in professional management, scientific advances in dairy development, and pragmatism and the results were great. Added to that was the social conscience, as we have called it our earlier work, *Reaching Out to the Poor* (Somjee and Somjee 1989). We shall illustrate the achievements of such cooperatives in different parts of India. Not all of them were able to keep to their initial position, as there were ups and downs in the development of most of them, including in the famous Amul Dairy. Then there were others, which came from behind, successfully fought against the bureaucratic stranglehold, and succeeded in several respects to get closer to the cooperative ideals established by the movement.

The stalwarts, who participated in building the cooperative movement from ground zero, often maintained that there would not have been a successful dairy movement in India had it not been for Amul; for that is where it all began. Amul not only established highly workable institutions at the district and grassroots levels, where none had existed before, but also provided a matrix within which the subsequent cooperative dairy development was cast. In that respect it also became a crucible or a container in which one could mix and experiment with what will be suitable for replication elsewhere.

Amul Dairy

In a literal sense, AMUL has been an offshoot of the Indian national movement. In its establishment, many top-flight national, state, and district level leaders were involved. To mention only the few: Sardar Patel, Morarji Desai, Tribhuvandas Patel, and countless others were deeply involved. So were some highly dedicated, innovative, and pragmatic technocrats such as Dr. V. Kurien and H. M. Dalaya. Their deep social concern for the Indian peasantry and, more specifically, the exploited section within it, became the central focus of the milk cooperative movement itself. These men were touched by something much bigger than themselves and found it extremely gratifying to work for the social goals embodied in that movement. What they started over half a century ago has spread to the rest of the country without losing sight of its original purpose, namely, to organize and protect the weaker social section with the help of cooperative institutions.

Over the years, more and more district milk unions came up in Gujarat and elsewhere that tried to continue or revive, at least in their formative years, the social idealism of the national movement period. No matter where you went in India, that was noticeable. The early days of dairy building brought out the best in the organizers, professionals, administrators, and even the politicians. Most of these organizations eventually became worldly with an awareness of economic realities and the need to compete. The best among them retained the social idealism of the early years and mixed it with economic realities of modern industry.

Those milk unions that combined vision and dedication with a realistic understanding of economic returns, did well. Farmers, managers, and professionals tackled their problems together, and jointly made crucial decisions of far-reaching significance. That, in a sense, was also the success of these organizations. They did not expect the idealism of the founding fathers to last forever. Underlying this there was also the realization, right down the line, that only the initial phase of a movement can be served by means of social idealism. After that, one must consider the "nitty-gritty" of economic well-being for all sections of people involved in cooperative dairying, and that, too, in a highly competitive world. This is precisely what the movement did. It rode the momentum of the early idealism generated by the Indian national movement. From then on, it put into place pragmatic policies and simple participatory procedures, as we shall see later, to make the cooperative institutions viable.

As the idealism generated by the Indian national movement gradually wore off, the rulers of independent India had to get down to solving the staggering problem of poverty in post-colonial India. Concerted efforts were needed in various fields. During the period immediately following independence, it was not anticipated that cooperative dairying would become as significant as it turned out to be in later years. The big players at that time were the state-run industries and services. They were expected to make a difference to poverty. But they achieved very little.

Such an insignificant beginning, with all eyes turned on the state-run institutions, also helped the cooperative movement find its bearings in the complex terrain of rural India. In 1946, a year before India's independence, it had succeeded in wrenching its independence from the bureaucracy of the Bombay state. It then set up the Amul Dairy in the city of Anand, which was destined to play a major role in the country. It soon got down to the task of collecting, pasteurizing, and marketing milk, which would guarantee better returns to its producers. It also provided veterinary services, cattle feed, dairy technology, management, and marketing know-how with the help of trained professionals. One of the remarkable things the movement did was build participatory grassroots cooperatives in villages, which would then send their elected representatives to district bodies in order to supervise the appointed staff consisting of professionals. Such a pattern of dairying, as we noted earlier, came to be known as the Anand Pattern. It was then replicated in the rest of the country with the help of the NDDB.

The establishment, consolidation, and replication of Amul greatly benefited from the social idealism generated by the Indian national movement. It had inspired not only the political workers, who came out of that movement and built cooperative institutions in rural communities, but also the management and the technical personnel right down the line. We began watching the operations of Amul since 1964, both in Anand and its adjoining rural communities, and were struck by the continued social idealism of the people who were involved. Three decades later in the mid-1990s, Amul, the flagship of the dairy industry, began to lose its idealism. The new generation of management that took over was more professional, desk-bound, and went about its business as organizational men and women. But by that time the cooperative movement in general, and Amul in particular, had deeply entrenched themselves in rural India.

Amul and its success inspired the birth of Dudhsagar in the neighboring district of Mehsana. They both came out of the Indian national movement and were firmly anchored in what it stood for. They started off with the support and dedication of their leaders and added to them professional management, research-minded, veterinary personnel, extension workers, etc., as they went along.

Each of them had their respective advantages. Amul had the services of a brilliant organization builder like Kurien, with his incomparable gift for building highly practical institutions that not only worked in rural areas, but also started yeilding results in the shortest possible time. Despite his highly modern outlook, he had a deep understanding of how he could interest the average farmer in the new institutions. His dedication to their welfare deeply ingratiated him, and we have come to know this first hand by visiting different parts of rural India over the last three decades. For Amul's day-to-day contact with milk producers, however, Kurien had to depend on T.K. Patel and several other social and political activists who came into the organization through the electoral mechanism. Kurien, the techno-manager, was able to strike a highly fruitful relationship with various politico-managers who came through the electoral process (Somjee 1983). But after him, that relationship became less and less harmonious. And what was worse, both sides had begun losing contact with the milk producers.

Dudhsagar Dairy

The same thing, however, did not happen to Dudhsagar. While there was no one comparable to Kurien in Dudhsagar, either in talents or institution-building capability, Dudhsagar excelled in a genuine and continuous contact with grassroots communities. Right down the line, from Chairman, to Managing Director, to General Manger, veterinarians etc., everyone spent a good part of their day either meeting the producers in villages or in their offices, preferably the former. Through its leading builders such as Motibhai Chaudhury, B.C. Bhatt, A.S. Dave, etc., Dudhsagar passed on the heritage of the Indian national movement to their colleagues and co-workers in grassroots communities. In them, and in their colleagues, one could see the spirit and social concern that one saw at the height of the national movement. Dudhsagar Dairy thus represented yet another dimension of the invaluable contribution the premier milk cooperatives of India made to the cooperative movement itself.

In all milk unions there were individuals who showed great concern and personal involvement in the work they were doing, but in Dudhsagar everybody did so from the time the organization came into being. Whether one took into consideration the top echelons of management, the veterinarians, the stockman, or the extension workers at the base, there was great personal involvement in what they were engaged in doing. And what is more, their focus always was on the neglected and the disadvantaged in grassroots communities. They did not stop at the formal definition of helping out the milk producers. They went out of their way to see that those with limited resources, and some times no resources of land or animals, were also able to join the milk producing community. Similarly, as we shall see in Chapter 3, they actively helped women play a more important role in managing milk cooperatives rather than confining them to the family cowshed.

Both Amul and Dudhsagar put a great deal of effort into attracting well-established agriculturists of their respective regions into dairying. Amul encouraged the Patidars while Dudhsagar concentrated on the Chaudhuries, who were also good breeders of animals. The Patidars were far more dynamic, were risk-takers, and were willing to try their hand at whatever offered good returns. At times they were involved in agriculture and dairying, and at other times in agriculture, commerce, and small-scale industry, all at the same time. As opposed to them, the Chaudhuries were far more committed to dairying. Dudhsagar's organizers realized this and helped them build a sizable income from dairying. Besides being good dairymen and dairywomen, the Chaudhuries were also given to teaching about it to the laborers in their cowsheds. Consequently, in Chaudhury dominated villages there was widespread interest in dairying from parts of the BCs, SCs, and tribals. Most of them had been apprentices in Chaudhury cowsheds.

The top leadership of Dudhsagar was, in fact, responsible for building the mega milk villages of the district. Its contact with them was beneficial to both. All of those villages had stories to tell about the frequent visits by the top leaders. Even veterinarians often turned their visits into mini village meetings. We watched the village of Pamol, a village that the senior veterinarian, A. S. Dave, used to visit frequently. In 1987, the village was struggling to reach the target of Rs.1 crore (10 million rupees or U.S.$222,222) from its milk procurement. Veterinarian A.S. Dave promised better animals, better artificial insemination straws, greater attention from his staff, more visits by him, etc., provided the village coop reach that coveted figure. When it actually did, he wanted them to see that more and more landless were turned into milk producers with the help of loans and cheaper fodder.

In the villages of Mehsana, there is a great human resource along with the famed milch animal, namely, the mesani buffalo. This human resource consists of Chaudhury women. All of their adult life is spent looking after their family and the animals in the cowshed. Over generations, where practical wisdom in dairying is handed down from mother to daughter, they have developed a rare kind of interest and expertise in taking care of animals and breeding them. Despite limited literacy, they were of great help to the research-minded veterinarians of Dudhsagar. Together, they perfected the mesani and are now on their way to developing not only cross-bred cows, but they are also going back to the indigenous animals to develop their milk giving capacity (Somjee 1989:106-111).

III. Targeting the Poor and Neglected

As discussed earlier, the dairies in Surat and Valsad, for pragmatic as well as idealistic reasons, targeted the tribals for dairy development in their respective districts. Here we shall mainly be concerned with the kinds of social activism that they brought into play in order to reach their goal. Their respective districts needed more milk than what the traditional suppliers of milk, namely, the middle caste agriculturists such as the Patidars and Desais, who were moving into bigger and better sources of income, could provide. They, therefore, had to build a milk producing peasantry out of a resourceless people such as the tribals. The variety of social activism that went into this pursuit will be of concern to us in this section.

Sumul Dairy

While Amul Dairy built its milk producing peasantry by concentrating on the agriculturists such as the Patidars, and Dudhsagar Dairy by modernizing the skills of the traditional breeders of animals such as the Chaudhuries, Sumul Dairy had to create, literally create, a new breed of milk producers from among its tribals who had neither animals nor experience in dairying. Initially, Sumul was forced to do it purely for pragmatic reasons. This is because over fifty percent of Surat district's population consists of tribals or adivasis. In its earlier years, Sumul Dairy built milk cooperatives in subdistricts that were heavily populated by Patidars and Desais, the two land-owning agricultural castes of the district. Even when irrigation was introduced to the district on a large scale, providing facilities for cash crops such as sugarcane, bananas, and other fruits and vegetables, these land-owning communities did not give up dairying. On the contrary, the increased availability of water and vegetation on their farms helped them support more milch animals.

But all that extra supply of milk was not enough for the booming city of Surat, which is a thriving center for textiles, art (synthetic) silk, diamond polishing, and extensive trade and commerce for South Gujarat in general. So, the question before Sumul was how to build milk cooperatives in adivasi villages with their very poor quality land and no milch animals worth the name. For their part, the adivasi villages, which for a long time had remained outside the mainstream economic life of the district, needed training and day-to-day supervisory help from socially concerned individuals. Response to such a need came from a highly dedicated team of veterinarians and social activists who came out of the independence movement and the Christian missionaries.

The response of adivasi villages, after initial skepticism, was phenomenal. By 1985, the veterinarians of Sumul, with the help of social activists in the district, had established 651 tribal milk cooperatives. By 1999, nearly 75 to 80 percent of Sumul's milk requirement was met with the help of milk coming from its adivasi villages. Thus, in less than two decades Sumul was able to bring tribal villages into the mainstream economic life of the district. In return, Sumul was also able to give back, on a regular basis, large sums of money to those villages. That, in turn, brought about far-reaching changes in the economic and social life of the people in those communities.

Since the adivasis were classed as an economically backward people, they were entitled to subsidies and loans for the purchasing of milch animals. As a result, it did not take them very long to become animal owners and milk producers. Moreover, the rate of return from Sumul was one of the most favorable among the dairies of Gujarat. Since the demand for milk in the city of Surat and its vicinity went up from 3 lakh (300,000) litres in 1985 to 6 lakh (600,000) litres in 1997, there was no difficulty in the sale of it. (Source: Sumul Dairy provided these figures).

Sumul was indeed fortunate to have a variety of socially concerned activists in its region who came together to transform the social and economic life of the adivasis. Principal among these were its own veterinary staff and, in particular, Dr. H.A. Ghasia. We went with him to many adivasi villages during our several field research visits, where he had built grassroots milk cooperative institutions. On the faces of the adivasis in those villages there was nothing but the expression of gratitude for him.

Ghasia's task was very much facilitated in the district by the presence of a large number of social activists who operated in South Gujarat. Some of them were the followers of Jayaprakash Narayan, JP as he was commonly known. They were disappointed with the results of Nehru's socialist policies. But more than that they were deeply apprehensive of the growing dictatorial nature of Indira Gandhi's rule. They therefore believed that Indians should be wary of the excesses of the indigenous rule. Such a government often tried to hide behind the fact that it was run by elected people. JP himself had come to the conclusion that those elected men and women of India were accountable to no one and that the state institutions and the bureaucracy, which they built, were simply self-serving. He therefore called on his followers to spread out over rural India and help farmers with their problems until such time as India set right its institutions by putting accountability at the center of democratic governance. A number of supporters of JP were operating in Surat district as NGOs. They also saw in cooperative dairying a partial realization of Mahatma Gandhi's constructive program. They were, therefore, most enthusiastic about working in adivasi villages, helping out with the management of grassroots cooperatives, and also training the adivasis to take over from them.

During the 1930s, Mahatma Gandhi had done the groundwork for social activists to operate in this region and beyond. One of his highly respected followers was Manibhai Desai. Gandhi wanted him to do similar work in the neighboring region of Maharashtra. Accordingly, Manibhai founded the well-known *ashram* in a village called Urlikanchan. He provided distinguished service to that village and to the surrounding region.

Finally, there was a regional thinker by the name of Jugatram Dave who believed that the social activists needed to have a clear understanding of the peculiarities of local problems in rural India and what it would take to solve them. Such social activists were therefore of inestimable value to the spread of cooperative dairying in rural Surat.

Also of great help in the operation of milk cooperative institutions in Surat district were the Spanish Christian missionary groups. As Ghasia's spearhead team moved from village to village in the district, it also needed help in training the adivasis to run the cooperatives. Ghasia's team trained a large number of them but could not reach all. The adivasis were a neglected group and most of the development plans and projects, launched by the state and central government since independence, had bypassed them. Sumul wanted to reverse that trend. It, therefore, not only established cooperative institutions in their villages, but also trained them to run those institutions. And since those institutions were tied to their livelihood, with the possibility of further economic advancement, the adivasis had to get involved in the operation of those institutions.

In some villages of the district, the Spanish missionaries shared that task. For that purpose, they themselves underwent training in Anand. The approach of Christian missionaries towards cooperatives underwent a change. Initially, they went to Anand where they were given a short course on how to help organize milk cooperatives. Father Iype from Kerala, and Father Caral from the Spanish mission, both of whom we had interviewed in early 1980s, were involved. When they returned back to Surat, they did outstanding work in adivasi villages. Initially, the Sumul Dairy staff was extremely pleased to have such assistance with their massive undertaking in the tribal belt. Later on, however, the same staff told us that the presence and towering personalities of the missionaries did not allow their indigenous leadership to assume a central role in organizing and managing the milk cooperatives. That there was no way the local leadership would advance unless it got involved in various participatory processes, committed mistakes, and learned through the process of trial-and-error.

The approach of the missionaries began to change in other parts of the rural areas, bordering on the district, called Bharuch district. There, father Berechi, of the same missionary organization, had done outstanding work along with a network of educational institutions. Unlike Iype and Caral, Berechi believed that the adivasis and their children needed good education and modern skills to prepare them for employment. Therefore you cannot simply concentrate exclusively on milk cooperatives and leave other facets of their development unattended.

Berechi, with his deeper understanding of the belief systems of the tribals, which he then synthesized with Christian religious practices, brought about a virtual revolution in the educational and economic development of a group of adivasi villages. Twice we looked at his work in the area and were amazed to see a cluster of modern educational institutions in the middle of nowhere. Boys and girls, from primary to higher secondary school, smartly dressed in their school uniform, attended their classes and played in their specially prepared playing fields. They showed great concern for their family and community, deeply identified themselves with national causes, and reflected a level of optimism for themselves and the country that was hard to find in other schools.

Berechi's achievements in the field of milk cooperative dairying were still more impressive. The group cooperative, which Berechi built and managed, was located across from the cluster of school buildings in a village called Nivalda, in the subdistrict of Dedia Pada. Since adivasi villages are often spread out into their fields, unlike other villages with a center, Berechi had to create a new center in Nivalda village with a milk-chilling center of its own.

The socially and educationally driven development process of the region of Dedia Pada had begun to spawn an economic growth of astounding proportions. Its milk cooperative society was registered in 1976 with 250 members. By 1997, its membership jumped to 4,000. In December 1997, the cooperative collected 14,500 litres per day. And, further, it had a chilling plant with a capacity for 33,500 litres.

The phenomenal rate at which the milk cooperative's income was rising was remarkable. Apart from the improved infrastructure of dairying, with cattle feed and artificial insemination facilities, it was also significant that the educated children were changing the thinking of their parents, particularly their mothers. Women were

Year	Milk Collection Per day (in litres)	Income from Milk
1994-95	3,684	Rs.1,49,43,252.88 (U.S.$332,072)
1995-96	4,900	Rs.1,96,56,689.48 (U.S.$436,815)
1996-97	10,700	Rs.3,11,38,182.93 (U.S.$691,959)
1997-98	14,500	Rs. Figures not available

Source: From the written records of the milk cooperative in Nivalda.

doing things that their educated children, now their leaders, wanted them to do. Hence, the holistic approach introduced by Berechi had begun to pay dividends. Moreover, he had concentrated on mass education, not just the education of the children of the adivasi's prominent families. This also meant that not all of them could go out of their rural communities to find employment in towns. That, in fact, had happened in other tribal communities where education was confined to the elite families. These communities had suffered setbacks because each time a young man or woman was educated, first thing he or she did was to go to work in towns. In contrast, Berechi's educated young men and women stayed in the village and helped build it economically and socially. Moreover, although Berechi had his own towering presence whenever he visited the Dedia Pada villages, the education of its young also prepared them to participate and develop themselves for leadership roles.

Two years later, when we visited the Nivalda village complex again, in the winter of 1999, it had made further progress in terms of its income from milk. Its income had gone up from Rs.3.1 crore (U.S.$691,959) to Rs.4.50 crores (U.S.$999,999) and was well set to hit five crores (U.S.$ 1.11m). In the year 2002-2003, it went well past it to Rs.6.04 crores (US$1.34m).

Another problem to attend to was that the adivasis were not ripped off by village shopkeepers, which they invariably were. The only way to stop that financial hemorrhage was to start a consumer cooperative at Nivalda itself where the adivasis could purchase articles of their daily need. Pressured by the shopkeepers of various villages, the state bureaucracy delayed giving permission for a consumer cooperative. Besides the more the adivasis progressed educationally and economically, the less likely they were to seek employment as majoors (laborers) as they had in the past. So, the rich farmers of upper castes joined with shopkeepers to delay the permission for a consumer cooperative. But in that, the vested interests were fighting a losing battle. For the younger generation of adivasis were not only educated, it was likely to raise awkward questions through the media and also through other political parties.

A similar development was taking place in yet another cluster of adivasi villages under a young Catholic Christian missionary from Goa by the name of Father Francis. His headquarters were in a village called Mandal. We revisited Mandal in the Songarh subdistrict of Surat, after nearly 15 years. In our earlier visit, Mandal had an Iype-Coral type missionary approach of shepherding the adivasis in everything. That had all changed. Father Francis was interested not only in the economic income of tribals from milk cooperatives, but was also keen on helping them to get the best education possible. But that was not all. He now wanted to give them health facilities. He was in charge of a hospital, with a doctor and trained nurses. Annually, the medical facility looked after more than 4,000 patients. It also helped to get rid of the widespread adivasi practice of consulting witch doctors.

In 1972, Mandal had a milk cooperative. In the year 2000, it had a cluster of schools and a hospital. Moreover, the hospital was the only medical facility available in a radius of 30 km. It had trained several health workers at the village level as well. There were missionary sisters, who were popularly known as Sisters of Vyara, who also had spent several years looking after the health of adivasis both in the Vyara and Mandal subdistricts. The holistic approach adopted by Father Francis had considerably improved the economic, education, and health situations of the people of the Songarh taluka, which, until recently, was considered to be one of the most backward subdistricts in Surat.

Social activism either preceding or accompanying the milk cooperative movement was no doubt evident in most of the rural communities where such a movement began. There were, however, instances where the very presence of social activists, even in unrelated fields such as education and health, also helped such a movement. One such rural community that we looked at was in the hills of Tamil Nadu in the south. The rural community of Yelagiri, consisting of 13 villages, came to have its milk cooperative in 1974, and in 1982 it opted to become an Anand Pattern milk cooperative.

With a population of about 8,500 people in 1999, its principal sources of income were milk and tourism.

Yelagiri also had two institutions either run or deeply influenced by Christian missionary organizations in the region. One was a school complex popularly known as Don Bosco school. The other was the Center For Rural Health and Social Education run by Dr. V. Benjamin and Dr. Sheila Benjamin. The latter was deeply influenced by the famous Vellore Christian Medical College, which has rendered an incomparable medical service to the region and outside.

The remarkable thing about Yelagiri was that the bulk of its population consisted of the OBCs and the STs who did not subscribe to Christian faith. And yet, these two Christian organizations prepared Yelagiri to get the maximum benefit from milk cooperative dairying by encouraging its leaders. Yelagiri thus represented yet another variety of social activism of the Christian institutions operating in India. Without constant encouragement from the leaders of these two organizations, dairying in these remote hill communities would not have done as well as it did.

Then there was social activism by leaders who rose from the grassroots communities as a result of their exposure to visiting dairy personnel. In the growth of such a leadership, the veterinarians and extension staff of Sumul had played an important part. Here we shall consider only two examples.

One of the prestigious tribal villages of Surat district is Anaval. It became well known for a variety of reasons. Apart from the fact that it is an overwhelmingly adivasi village, and its milk cooperative came up in the shortest possible time, it has also produced a local leadership of a high caliber and dedication. The Sumul veterinarians played a major role in building this leadership. Earlier, the leadership had confined itself to organizing forest workers' associations so as to protect tribals from ruthless contractors. This led to a wider debate on how to protect the adivasis of the region from other forms of exploitation. Since the land they owned was of poor quality, those adivasis were forced to work as forest workers. Therefore, they desperately needed an alternative source of livelihood. When Sumul brought the milk cooperative to their doorstep, the local leadership enthusiastically welcomed it. By way of initial groundwork, Sumul had to do very little. The local leadership was able to organize everything. The adivasi cohesiveness, together with the willingness of its leadership to work for its people, got the cooperative institutions going in the shortest possible time.

Established in 1972, with a meager milk collection of 17 litres a day, in 1999 it collected 3,200 litres a day, and remained at the top of the 68 milk cooperatives within the subdistrict. This resulted in a steady income for the village, which was continually growing.

In the year 2004, its milk collection went up to 3,500 litres a day. It also installed a computer and a chilling plant to eliminate the problem of milk sourage. The milk cooperative of Anaval, in the same year, started ploughing back Rs.65,000 (U.S.$1,444) per day into its economy. The village high street now has the look of a boomtown. Anawal a tribal village, had created a per capita member income of Rs.52,000 (U.S.$1,115) per year. And it was able to generate that income in a span of 32 years.

One of its leaders, Gambhirbhai Parmar, who had spent close to thirty years building the institution, paid great attention to building its second line of leadership. He himself had come under the influence of the JPians who believed that much work needed to be done at the base of Indian society. The arrival of the milk cooperative in the village thus gave him an opportunity to do precisely that. In a span of thirty years, Anaval was transformed from a sleepy little adivasi village into a small township, with schools, transport facilities, shops, and the possibility of a health center. The adivasis invested their income in building better dwellings (some of them with indoor plumbing), expanding their cattle holding, improving land for agriculture, and preparing their children for good education, new skills, and professions. Like the upper class residents of the district who aimed at going to America, the Anavalians dreamed of the same. Even the local postman, it was reported, had finally ended up in America and was regularly sending his "letters from America" to his relatives and friends back home. Thanks to the milk cooperative dairy and local leadership, Anaval was on the move.

While Sumul's staff could not reach all the adivasi villages, and there were more than six hundred of them in the district, the educated among the adivasis themselves sometimes built milk cooperatives on their own initiatives. A village called Gantoli, in Mandavi taluka in Surat district, was one such village. A family with two generations of school teachers in it, thought that it should do something for the village over and above teaching its children. So it approached Sumul and with its help established a milk cooperative in the village. The steady income from milk transformed the village's standard of living in the shortest possible time. Even women felt indebted to the teachers and, in return, vowed to educate themselves. So, while the older generation of women came to acquire education equivalent to primary standard, the younger ones came up to the seventh standard and beyond. Through the mediation of the milk cooperative, and also the family of teachers, the village paid back in kind its founders, a teacher family, by pursuing education. The members of that family narrated to us with great pride what they did for the village, and how it paid them back. Thus, the district of Surat abounds in many forms of social activism coming from a variety of sources.

Vasudhara Dairy

This then brings us to the case of Vasudhara Dairy in the adjoining district of Valsad, the staff of which pursued some of the most idealistic goals known to dairy circles and got the best of results out of them. As stated earlier, Valsad district, like Surat, was also overwhelmingly tribal in its population. Its decision to hand over the newly constituted milk cooperatives to tribal women, followed by an increase in milk productivity, and the subsequent winning of productivity prizes, attracted a lot of attention in the cooperative community across India.

For the organizers of Vasudhara, putting women in charge was not just an act of faith. It was, on the contrary, the most practical thing to do. From their point of view, dairying was an economic activity in which women were already deeply involved. So, why not train them in modern methods of dairying and thereby achieve the desired result in the shortest possible time?

One of the founding fathers of Vasudhara was Narendrabhai Vashibhai, popularly known as Vashibhai, who possessed a combination of the social activism of South Gujarat and the NDDB's highly practical use of modern technology. He also had a common-sense approach, believing that since women do the work of dairying in any case, along with other chores around the house, it is fitting that they should be put in charge of it without compartmentalization of responsibilities. The entire development of the dairy industry should therefore be routed through them, and that they should be trained, continually, for new developments and responsibilities. He was thus able to persuade his colleagues of the need to have a four-fold approach: social activism; modern technology; viable economic institutions; and women in charge.

Vashibhaibhai's colleagues, and especially his fieldworkers and extension officers, enthusiastically welcomed this approach. We watched his staff over a period of two years, both in their office locations and in villages, and were amazed to see how very devoted they were to their goals. Theirs was a kind of a staff-coordinated social activism. Most of them barely had any family life of their own. They worked late, and for seven days a week. Such a devotion to work in rural India reminded one of the early days of Indian independence. The tribal women also responded enthusiastically to the trust put in them. Whether in adopting new techniques of dairying, applying for loans for building the herds, or launching micro-credit groups, or sanitation, the tribal women of Valsad stood behind the organizers/social activists with great enthusiasm and implemented various proposals in the shortest possible time. They worked as a team, and with great speed.

On his part, Vashibhaibhai believed that if an average adivasi family is provided with three cross-bred cows, its annual income would be in the vicinity of Rs.35,000 (U.S.$777). That amount, in addition to some agricultural income, would give the household a comfortable start. From then on, it would have to make a choice on whether to have more animals or start a small commercial venture in a nearby town. Most of the rural communities, so far, have expressed their preference for continuing with dairying rather than become involved in other forms of investment.

Apart from their hardworking disposition, these women also brought an adaptive approach to their work. Unlike other traditional lower social groups in India, in particular the former untouchables, the adivasis, having been outside the framework of traditional Hindu social hierarchy, were able to escape the bruises, humiliations, and a sense of insignificance. It was, therefore, easier to mold them into a resource for economic development. The building of the lower castes as an economic resource, on the other hand, required a different strategy. Vasudhara had hoped that if the adivasis came on board, they would then act as role models to help raise the other disadvantaged groups from poverty.

In Gujarat, the home of people with a highly developed economic acumen, it was unnecessary to emphasize the need for cooperatives to become commercially viable organizations. Vasudhara's social activist staff believed that even a cooperative must stand on its own economic feet. In that sense, its social agenda should occupy a subordinate position. Its overall strategy was to become viable as an economic organization first and then reinvest profits into social projects. Curiously, since it dealt with the economically and socially backward communities, its social agenda also became good business. It was able to build, in its members, a rare kind of enthusiasm and commitment to serve the economic goals of the organization. Vasudhara, like Sumul, was able to pursue its social agenda side by side with its economic agenda, putting them in a continuing symbiotic relationship in which each helped the other.

In the year 2000, Vasudhara launched an ambitious program to make ice-cream. For that purpose it bought an ice-cream plant in a town called Boisar, which is across the border in Maharashtra state. In order to avoid duty and interstate hassle, it brought milk from Valsad, which is in Gujarat state, but made ice-cream in Maharashtra state and marketed it as Amul ice-cream in the metropolis of Mumbai. It then installed, in 2003, another ice-cream plant in Maharashtra state's second largest city called Nagpur. The cover of this book carries a picture of its Boisar ice-cream plant.

IV. From Governmentalism to Cooperatism

Kolhapur milk union earned the admiration of the community of cooperatives for its near painless switch from a government-run cooperative to a self-governing Anand Pattern cooperative. One of the factors that assisted such a switch was the deeply ingrained tradition of social activism in the state of Maharashtra. Such a tradition had touched not only its social workers, but also the bureaucrats. While its social workers like Anand Rao Patil, who went from village to village persuading members of grassroots cooperatives to opt for the Anand Pattern, its equally committed bureaucrats gave a helping hand in building the adequate infrastructure for such a change. In the final analysis, no argument was more persuasive than the better price that the milk union was able to get for its product when it was released from government control.

But Kolhapur milk union had another fight on its hands. Its switch from governmentalism to cooperatism was easier than the fight in providing a common grassroots cooperative to all its members. In the latter it was up against the social division of castes and untouchability. To this day, that fight is not yet over.

There is a deeply rooted, local, social hierarchy among the agriculturists of Kolhapur district. Locally, these agriculturists are known as Patils. They came into power after the Brahmins and the Marathas. Once in power, they claimed to be the descendents of one of the great heroes of Maharashtra, namely, Shivaji and his descendants. Preceding such a claim, they had also launched a movement towards social equality that was mainly directed against the Brahmins. Unfortunately, that movement did not extend to the Dalits or the former untouchables who constituted a large proportion of district's population. Recently, some of them even embraced Buddhism in order to escape the humiliation of untouchability.

The Gokul milk union at Kolhapur, as it is called, with all its social activism, was unable to help the Dalits in their social mobility. It could not persuade the Marathas and Patils to be fair-minded towards the Dalits. Those two castes, having won their battle for social dignity against the Brahmins, were not willing to concede the same to the Dalits. Such a social problem started manifesting itself in the milk cooperatives. While Kolhapur was able to shake off feudalism and governmentalism, it could not provide equality to the Dalits as far as the membership of cooperatives was concerned.

For a prolonged period, the Congress Party ruled the state of Maharashtra by cleverly manipulating the cleavages between the Marathas, Patils, and Dalits. Of the three, the Patils of Maharashtra registered the fastest economic, educational, and professional development. They also became the political elite of the district. Neither the Marathas nor the Patils were keen on allowing the Dalits to become members of milk cooperatives. Consequently, the only way Kolhapur could help the Dalits to become members was to allow them to have their own parallel institutions in villages throughout the district.

While Kolhapur did come to have Anand Pattern cooperatives, what it did not have was a socially integrated cooperative institution for its milk producers. This was despite the fact that Maharashtra, more than Gujarat, had been the home of several social activists who had worked assiduously in its rural areas helping the socially disadvantaged. But at every stage the Marathas and/or the Patils resisted treating Dalits as their equals in the milk cooperatives.

Consequently, within the district there are at least 400 villages that have two milk cooperatives, one for the Dalits and the one for the rest. The NDDB staff must have called at least 100 meetings to integrate them, but so far it has not had much success. The Dalits of Maharashtra, who deeply agonized over the resistance of the upper castes, are now an angry group of people seeking wider social justice and not just the formality of a common membership. So, while Kolhapur milk cooperatives have helped the Dalits to improve their economic condition, they have not been able to help them overcome the social injustices that were imposed by the traditional social organization. As of now, having two separate cooperatives has been the only practical solution. And as far as the Dalits are concerned, they want to fight out the battle for social equality and respect for their dignity in courts and in elections and force Kolhapur to amalgamate its parallel grassroots cooperatives.

V. Poverty and the Role of Social Activists

One of the misconceptions concerning poverty alleviation is that once opportunities are created for the poor, the poor will necessarily seize those opportunities and rise out of poverty. Depending on the nature of opportunities created, there always will be segments of the poor who cannot, by themselves, make use of such opportunities. Often, they will need help from what we have called "human intermediaries," initially, to make use of those opportunities (Somjee and Somjee 1989:136). This is because as groups or individuals they may be so devastated, in human terms, they may not always believe that those opportunities are for them. Social indignities or continued exclusion from the mainstream social and economic life, as was the case with India's former untouchables and tribals where a large number of poor are located, often created a view among them that India's development plans were only for its economically privileged. The poor, therefore, needed the help of social activists to teach them about those opportunities and help them make use of what had been provided for them. This was the role played by various social activists in specific fields of cooperative dairying.

Let us now examine the reality of what the milk cooperatives and social activists have been able to do for the rural poor. As a rule, membership in the bulk of milk cooperatives is open to the rural poor, some of whom lack land or dairy animals or both. Two decades ago, the top leadership of milk cooperatives seemed defensive whenever we put the question to them, "what are you doing for the poor?" Their answer, invariably, was, "nobody can help those who are without sadhan" (which means land or cattle). This is no longer the case. What one hears instead is that if the government is willing to give them subsidy, and banks to lend them the remaining amount by way of loans, they, the organizers, would collect money in installments from milk income and repay it to the banks. There are some cooperative institutions, however, that say outright that they do not want the headache of collecting this money. Mercifully, these are declining in number.

Of equal significance is the changing pattern of rural wages, particularly in areas where there is irrigation or a reasonable availability of water. In such areas, the landless laborers often insist on being given farm cuttings as part of their wages. In Gujarat this is called bharo, or the head load of farm cuttings. The going wage rate for landless laborers is often a matter of local supply and demand, but the bharo privilege is often built into it. Occasionally, one may find a landowner who might ask for a share in the bharo, but these are few and far between. The landless laborer can supplement wages with the help of specially prepared cattle feed to maintain a milch animal and create an additional income for himself/herself. We have known in Surat district examples of landless laborers not only supplementing their income, but also building a pukka (brick) house for themselves on the roadside land, which they can buy at a reasonable rate. In Mehsana district there are villages with fodder farms on the village common where the landless can work and obtain bharo at a reasonable rate. The well-known village of Pamol, as discussed earlier, is one of them. Truly, rural poverty, which until recently was considered a problem of the unfortunate, is now seen as neglect on the part of politicians, officials, the village community, and/or milk cooperatives that are ostensibly there to help them.

In their early years the milk cooperatives did not make a distinction between the milk producers and the poor as such. From them, the fact that all milk cooperatives called themselves "producers' cooperatives" meant that if one did not have animals, one was not their concern. Only those who produced milk were worthy of attention. This perception has gradually changed.

Traditionally speaking, the poor thought of themselves as the wards or the moral responsibility of the rich. After independence, the notion was that the poor were the responsibility of powerful politicians or ministers or the government. This was then followed by a reworked definition of what constituted good government: a good government was one that helped the poor in addition to the other duties it performed. But when more than four decades of Congress Party "socialism" pushed more and more people below the poverty line, the responsibility for helping the poor fell on

socially concerned individuals and institutions. The milk cooperatives thus inherited India's poor because no one else, with the
possible exception of some social activists, wanted them. When the
two joined hands, they made a difference. Within the network of
milk cooperatives, right from the apex body such as the NDDB
down to the milk unions in the districts and the village level milk
cooperatives, there were always some individuals who combined
their professional work as administrators, veterinarians, dairymen,
engineers, etc., with deep social commitment. During our field
research, which was conducted almost entirely at the village level,
we had the privilege of watching such individuals at work. These
were the human intermediaries who often led the diffident poor to
new provisions and opportunities. And their efforts almost always
produced results.

Such individuals came from various institutions, ranks, and
areas of specialization. They built a core of workers around themselves who had deeply internalized their social concern. Kurien and
T.K. Patel, in the early and difficult days of cooperative movement,
displayed these qualities. Their social concerns and skills influenced
their colleagues. Later on, Kurien in the NDDB and Motibhaibhai
Chaudhury in Dudhsagar assumed similar roles. While Kurien and
his successor Amrita Patel built a dedicated army of professionals
with a deep social conscience, Motibhai Chaudhury performed a
cooperative miracle in the arid lands of Mehsana to prove that you
can do a lot for the poor with a combination of skill, professionalism, and a committed social conscience.

A still greater achievement in directly helping the poor was
accomplished by Sumul and Vasudhara. They converted their
districts' adivasi population into milk producers. The adivasis of
India, because of historical and social reasons, were left out of the
mainstream economic life of the country. Sumul's veterinarians, in
particular Dr. H.A. Ghasia, with a deep social concern for helping

these left out people, achieved astounding results. Similarly, the neighboring Vasudhara dairy, with the same composition of adivasi population, went a step further. Under the leadership of its top organizers, such as Vashibha, Suresh Desai, and Bina Desai, adivasi women were able to raise their own standard of living and go beyond dairying to micro saving, sanitation, education, etc. So far, these organizers have not been able to help a landless group called the Halpatis, who work as farm laborers on the farms of the Patidars and Desais. But given their success with the adivasis, they should induct, before long, the Halpatis into dairying.

The Halpatis of the district, still remain one of the major challenges for the social activists of both Sumul and Vasudhara dairies. The task of the social activists becomes more difficult because the Halpatis do not have much land, unlike the adivasis. Moreover, they have worked as farm laborers on the farms of Patidars and Desais for a long time. They, therefore, have lost the will and courage to try something different.

The dynamics of the agriculturist communities of the district have recently presented the Halpatis with an unexpected opportunity. The prosperous landowning communities of some of the subdisticts of Surat have emigrated to the United States or Britain, leaving behind elderly relatives to look after their property with the help of Halpatis. This was the condition in 2003-2004 of the agricultural properties of Desais and Patidars in the subdistricts of Bardoli, Olpad and Pulsana in Surat District. Over-dependence on Halpatis had improved their wage structure, enhanced their residential facilities and domestic work for their women. It is not certain how long such an unexpected bonanza for the Halpatis will last.

Twenty-five years ago, one could see a lot of poverty in the villages of Surat district. Now it is much less. According to astute observers of the local scene there are three reliable indicators of it: meals twice a day, reasonably good clothing, and children in schools. And this is what is evident today in Surat and Valsad districts.

Sumul's concentration on the adivasis had helped them go beyond a regular income from milk to a possible additional agricultural income from sugarcane. Earlier, the irrigation department had ignored the needs of the poor of the district. Ukai Dam, in the district, supplied water to the Desais and Patidars in far away lands but not to adivasis' fields which were barely 20 kilometers away. But this time around, the funds generated by milk, especially for adivasi households, helped them to install pumps and other irrigation devices to get water and then grow sugarcane in their own backyard. And what is more, they now (2001-2002) grow nearly 40 percent of district's sugarcane. Furthermore, steady income from milk has also given the adivasis a good credit rating and now banks trust them with loans. Moreover, the adivasis themselves have become saving-minded.

Being on the margin of Hindu society, the adivasis, unfortunately, cannot escape its hierarchical influence. Consequently, what were, until recently, largely horizontal groups in terms of social status, are now beginning to arrange themselves in a hierarchical position of Dholia Patel, Chaudhuries (tribals), Gamits, Vasavas, usually in that order. At this stage, however, such a hierarchy reflects, to a large extent, their respective success in the economic field. But within each of these adivasi groups, there is the likelihood of yet another hierarchy that will shuffle their status on the lines of entrepreneurship, profession, and the nature of employment.

Banas Dairy in Sabarkantha district presented yet another picture of the relationship between the landless and milk cooperatives. Since it was a drought-stricken district, there was no question of the landless claiming the privilege of bharo along with their agricultural wage. Consequently, if the landless wanted to become milk producers, they had to buy fodder as well as prepared cattle feed and make a strict commercial "go" of their undertaking. Very few landless, therefore, came into the milk producing community. Most of the landowners, who employed them at Rs.40 per day (1999), did not allow farm cuttings. Those who did, took away half the portion for their own animals. These landless people largely belonged to the Dalit category. While there was a possibility of their getting subsidy for buying animals, there always was a problem of feeding them.

Let us now examine a few examples, across the states, where the landless made it on their own with minimum help from social activists. Among the landless in Banas, the only group to prosper was the Venkars. Since their traditional occupation of weaving required them to make use of animal gut, they got classified as Dalits. However, they never forgave the upper castes for this. Consequently, they worked hard, became educated, and made good use of social legislation, which helped to uplift them. They got jobs as teachers, office workers, and shop assistants. The older men and women among them, however, continued to do physical labor on the condition that during monsoon season they would be allowed to have farm cuttings. This, along with cattle feed, helped them to maintain animals. Since the bulk of them were educated, they saw to it that they always bought high milk-yielding crossbred cows. They combined their extraordinary self-help attitude with whatever provisions were there in education, employment, loans, and subsidy for getting animals, and then rose out of poverty and resourcelessness. While the other lower castes envied the Vankars throughout Gujarat, the upper castes paid them grudging respect for being better educated than themselves and also for holding positions of steady income such as school teachers, nurses, and office secretaries.

One of the agriculturally prosperous districts in the south is Erode in Tamil Nadu. We looked at the problems of milk cooperatives there from the point of view of interference by the state government to fix the price of milk largely to favor urban voters. As a result, the Erode milk union was not able to collect more than 20 percent of milk in the district. That, however, did not discourage the poor. The shortage of labor in the district meant that they were paid good wages. And they thus combined the two sources of income and remained the staunchest supporters of cooperative dairying.

Even within such a group of landless pourers of milk, there were aspirations for upward economic mobility. For some in Tamil Nadu, there is a tie between investment in more milch animals or power looms. One could get a milch animal for Rs.12,000 (U.S.$266) to 15,000 (U.S.$333). But a power loom would cost Rs.100,000 (U.S.$2,222). And if he/she has Rs.25,000 (U.S.$ 555) by way of down payment, and an enterprising disposition, the bank would give a loan for the remaining Rs.75, 000 (U.S.$1,666) for a power loom. And the borrower can pay off that amount in five to six years. But even as a loom operator, the borrower can keep at least one milch animal, send spouse and possibly grown up children to work in fields, and operate the power loom.

A similar pattern of upward mobility was found in the villages of Karnataka where the landless laborers keep at least one milch animal but invest their savings in silk worms. In a comparison of milk and silk, there is a great margin of profit in the latter, though there is also an amount of risk. That risk can be balanced with the help of a milch animal and family income can be supplemented by sending women to work on farms. Similarly, one of the poorest districts in the south, namely, Dharampuri on the border of Karnataka and Tamil Nadu, has its landless people trying to supplement their dairy income, which is regular, with a more uncertain income from poultry. Until recently, birds died of unknown diseases and therefore poultrying was considered to be a risky investment, despite a good profit margin on that investment.

One of the desperately poor and ill-governed states of India is Bihar. It was not always that way. It has India's 40 percent mineral wealth and enviable water facilities, which can sustain a large number of milch animals. But due to caste conflicts, administrative mismanagement, violence, and corruption, it is now categorized as a "sick state." It has a large number of desperately poor people in it and there was a question if milk cooperative dairying would succeed there and, more specifically, provide an escape route from poverty. Surprisingly, milk cooperatives were able to make a little bit of progress where nothing else worked. This was largely due to the dedication of a highly trained team sent by the NDDB and also, to some extent, the grassroots leaders who saw the benefits to be obtained from milk cooperatives. Some of the attractions that they offered to their rapidly growing milk producing community, drawn largely from lower agriculturist castes such as the Yadavs, were subsidies and loans, veterinary services, good price for milk, and, above all, corruption-free, regular payments. The landless laborers, because of the greenery around, started claiming bharo privileges where they worked. The Yadavs as well as the landless knew that their effort at building milk cooperatives, and prospering through them, would require them to insulate themselves from the local political infighting and the corrupt practices of politicians. So they too gave a hand to the NDDB team to operate milk cooperative institutions uninfluenced by political considerations.

The problem of rural poverty in relation to cooperative dairying in different parts of India thus needs to be looked at with reference to the specific regional situation within which it is located.

VI.   Some General Observations

The milk cooperatives of India had to depend on human and mate-rial resources, leadership, social activism, and grassroots responses that were available in each of the districts in which they operated. The availability of fodder and the quality of animals were, no doubt, basic to the success of those institutions. But equally important were the vision, commitment, and drive of its district level leadership. In some districts, it did not take much to pump life into the local peas-antry. It was already there, requiring an initial push and an adequate set of institutions within which it could operate. In the case of Amul and, later on, Dudhsagar, some extra effort was no doubt needed because there was not enough experience with building milk cooperatives along modern lines. They were the pioneers. But both those cooperatives were fortunate to have the services of some of the greatest leaders of the Indian dairy movement. Moreover, in their respective districts, they also had human resources that were touched by the Indian national movement, which had brought out the best in them. Such resources proved to be of inestimable value because of their commitment, social activism, and determination to overcome problems in establishing grassroots institutions.

With Sumul and Vasudhara came some of the boldest experiments in cooperative dairying. Sumul took milk cooperatives to the adivasis of the district and Vasudhara brought their womenfolk into cooperative dairying with a determination to let them handle the milk economy. Both experiments produced great results. Their entire effort, however, would not have seen the light of the day had there not been a tradition of social activism in their respective districts. The social activists not only brought in economic benefits, but also transformed the outlook of these two organizations toward dairying itself. The dairying, no doubt, was primarily an economic activity. But once that was achieved, the benefits of it could serve a variety of social goals. With the help of social activists, therefore, cooperative dairying came to acquire a social purpose, which was not there in the earlier years of the movement.

With Sabar and Banas, which operated in highly unfavorable environmental conditions, we had examples of the triumph of human spirit and endeavor in building institutions that could give refuge to farmers who were forced to switch from agriculture to dairying because of the adverse climatic conditions. The milk cooperatives rescued farmers from destitution, saved their animals, and provided them with alternative means of income during lean years. All this tested their managerial skills to the utmost.

Then there were the milk cooperatives in various parts of India where milk technocrats, social activists, and Christian missionary groups worked long and hard to help the uninitiated learn how to operate participatory institutions.

Finally, the social activists involved in the movement were also responsible for broadening its focus from "milk producers" to the "poor." Unlike the milk economy in the countries of the West, milk cooperatives of India, under the leadership of social activists, genuinely became institutions of the small and marginal farmers, and also of the poorest of the poor. In a genuine sense, then, the movement provided an escape route from poverty for those whom it touched.

Social activists, regardless of where they came from, had a problem of retiring from their active involvement in whatever they were doing. Some of them refused to retire despite advancing age. They genuinely believed that they still had quite a lot to offer, and that retirement should not come in their way. Others were called back after retirement because their institutions needed their guidance to train the next generation. Still there were others who successfully found a new suitable niche to work in, given their advancing age. In these post-retirement profiles one thing was clear: it was not very easy for any one of them to walk away from the gripping human drama of poverty alleviation in which they had played the role of the principal alleviator. The poor needed them as much as they needed the poor. Under the circumstances all the limits of retirement seemed arbitrary and at times cruel.

Chapter 3

Redoing the Gender Equation

In most cultures women have been the last to be recognized as a disadvantaged group and no society, developed or developing, has so far been able to do away, completely, with all their disadvantages. Until 1971, even Switzerland did not think that women were worthy of the vote. Women in the Canadian civil service had to fight a prolonged legal battle to get equal pay for equal work, and that was not won until a few years ago. The United States has yet to elect its first woman president. Until recently, the most prestigious universities of Britain, such as Oxford and Cambridge, would not admit women into their well-known colleges. Finally, India has yet to take seriously what is called "the shame of missing women," whereby the ratio of women to men has been reduced to 933 per every 1,000 men (India Office of the Registrar General 2001).

Throughout the world enlightened men and women, together with social activists, have denounced the disadvantages heaped on women. They have been joined in this effort by the media, the judiciary, and international development agencies. Mahatma Gandhi criticized the holy text of the Hindus, namely, the *Manu Smurti*, for making women subservient to men. But he did not stop there. He developed one of the most effective programs to deal with women's disadvantages and that was to involve women in social and political movements so that through such activities they could grow in their political capacity and demand what is rightfully theirs. In building women's political capacity, Gandhi had shown a rare insight into the problem of "redoing the gender equation." For him, legal provisions for women's rights were necessary only as a starting point. If women were to stop there then they would forever depend on bureaucrats and courts to secure what has been legally provided.

It is equally necessary for women to get involved in legal and political *processes* whereby they can secure what is rightfully theirs. Women also need to overcome their own deeply internalized sense of insignificance; a diminished sense of self-worth that will not be discarded until they get involved in social and political processes and keep reminding themselves that they too are of equal worth and importance to their society.

On the topic of opportunities for women to get involved in social and economic processes, there is a question whether the milk cooperatives of India, which came to their doorstep in grassroots communities, helped them directly, indirectly, or not at all.

Conceptually, the approach of cooperative organizers at the district or union level had evolved in the following manner. Initially they treated women as *targets*, whereby the expectation was to involve more of them in different functions of the dairy industry of which they were the unacknowledged managers. So, it was logical to pass on more work to them. Later, women were seen as *conduits*, through which various changes in the domestic cowshed could be implemented. The animal artificial insemination drive, a massive switch to crossbred cows, and animal healthcare generally, were all routed through women. Simultaneously, there was also an emphasis on the involvement of women because men were perceived to be less compliant to the policies of organizers than women. Furthermore, women were seen as less prone to treating milk cooperatives as a stepping-stone to their larger political ambitions or goals than men.

Throughout such explorations into what ought to be the appropriate roles for women, the overarching goal of the dairy organizers remained the same, and that was how to increase milk collection for the cooperatives. It is toward this goal that women would prove to be most useful. Without involving themselves in any ambitious program of narrowing the gender distance, the organizers wanted women as allies in search of greater productivity and procurement. Very few of them expected women to grow in their participatory and, in some cases, political capacity, and then turn around and make a few demands of their own. For quite sometime, organizers did not anticipate that women would emerge as, what we would like to call, *critical agents,* who would not only be crucial to milk cooperative dairying, but would also make some demands of their own. In other words, as critical agents they sometimes went beyond what the organizers had anticipated or were willing to offer. At such times, the organizers had to rethink their strategies and responses.

In this chapter we shall illustrate the changing perception of the organizers towards women and also women's discovery of the importance of their own participation in the cooperatives. We shall illustrate this with the help of our grassroots findings in different regions. The evolution of the organizers' perceptions of women, from *targets* to *conduits* to *critical agents,* is central to our understanding of how the gender equation in milk cooperatives was reshaped. In different parts of India, the organizers had been caught off guard when women started making different demands on them, some new, some unexpected, and some highly challenging.

Even when women were treated as targets for development, the idea was to use them, by and large, either as a means to increasing milk productivity, as troubleshooters, or as a counterweight to men wanting to expand their political space. One of the major worries connected to milk cooperatives was how they could be used for political gain for the men who presided over them. Those men who got involved in electoral politics of the state or the center were discreetly told not to involve the cooperative institutions in their political contests. As long as the Congress Party ruled the country and most of its states, it clandestinely influenced the organizers to let it indirectly use those institutions. Moreover, the Congress, as a *movement* (though not as a party), was also responsible for the social activism of rural India since before independence. But as the Congress faced more and more challenges from other political parties, and also diminished in its social activist role, milk cooperatives wanted to steer clear of it and other political parties. And as women were considered to be less politically ambitious and less amenable to manipulation by political parties, they were seen as making cooperatives as apolitical and unresponsive to outside influences as possible.

Dairying in India was increasingly perceived as gender specific, and women were expected to shoulder the responsibility for a large range of dairy activity, including decision-making and leadership. In western and southern India they were seen as indispensable to the perennial problem of rural credit. So, an obvious answer was to train them for all kinds of functions and roles.

The women, as we shall see in this chapter, came to have a mind and an agenda of their own. In western India, they forced Amul to provide healthcare services not only to their animals, but also to their families. In Andhra Pradesh they fought against elected politicians of the state for running a private dairy of their own with the help of milk cooperative staff. In Rajasthan they made life difficult for the organizers for not making an effort to cooperatize the sale of agricultural commodities over and above milk. And in Kolhapur they repeatedly pointed out the shame of having two sets of milk cooperatives, one for the Dalits and the other for the rest of the people.

In the following pages, we shall go into these and other related issues. This chapter is divided into the following subsections: (I) Women as Targets and Conduits; (II) Women as Trained Co-Contributors; (III) Women as Critical Agents; and finally, (IV) Self-Involvement as a Means to Women's Ethnodevelopment.

I. Women as Targets and Conduits

During the heyday of Amul in the 1970s, the question was: although the institution was, no doubt, helping small and marginal farmers, along with medium and large farmers, was that enough? While small and marginal farmers, including Venkars (former untouchables), started to derive benefits from the grassroots milk cooperatives, had everyone who was *disadvantaged* for reasons of caste and class been covered? Who had been left out? The answer: women. Women had been left out of this great enterprise, and that was neither fair nor good. Furthermore, if women were placed in important positions, it would look better for the organization. At the same time, one could not wait indefinitely for the women to come to the organization and say please make a cooperative for us. The cooperative would have to reach out to them.

Precisely at that time a Brahmin widow showed up at the doorstep of Amul asking for the establishment of a cooperative in her village because her fellow women had to go more than three kilometers to pour milk in another village. During winter evenings, especially, when it got dark early, it was not convenient. The answer of the mid-level decision-makers was "no," because her village was too close to the other village, which already had a cooperative. When the dejected woman was about to leave, she was asked to consider the possibility of having a women's cooperative instead; the proximity of the other cooperative would not be a problem. They asked if she would call a general body meeting of her village and make a formal application to Amul to that effect? In the beginning the woman was terrified and said that the village women had no such experience but she would certainly try. When the village meeting was duly held and the necessary paperwork was completed, Amul agreed to have the district's first women's cooperative. The name of the village is Khadgodhara. We were able to study this village and publish our observations (Somjee and Somjee 1978). With constant encouragement from Amul, and village-level women's leadership, the milk cooperative of Khadgodhara became very productive. After a few years, however, women from different ethnic and religious groups took over, and the cooperative lacked cohesion. Apart from internal dissension among women, the men from the upper castes, in particular, did not forgive women for competing for political power. A number of women veterans of the cooperative, after a brief stint, had contested elections for the *panchayat* (village council), which, until recently, had been the preserve of men. So, what the men wanted now was a compliant group of women in the cooperative who would also keep their noses out of panchayat politics. And they succeeded. The asymmetrical male-female relationship in the domestic situation was reflected in the public life of the village.

As far as Amul was concerned, Khadgodhara was just a flash in the pan and not a product of its changing perception of women. It regularly brought women from different villages to tour its highly impressive pasteurization plant in Anand. The women were routinely showed the different processes of milk pasteurization. Then women were able to view, through a microscope, animal semen for cross-fertilization with all its living cells. This would be followed by a good lunch, a pep talk on the importance of their contribution, and then the buses would head home. Away from their domestic chores, the women were always happy to make those trips and repeatedly asked their village cooperatives when they would again be allowed to visit Amul. Simultaneously, Amul's extension department tried to create a better understanding among women about the character of cooperatives by addressing meetings in each village with songs about cooperatives and sentences that the women were supposed to complete with a collective chant. The message was that the cooperative "belonged" to them and that they were its true creators, sustainers, and beneficiaries. Implicit in those practices was the emerging point of view of Amul, where women were the key to greater productivity in milk, and therefore cooperatives at all levels should target them and also give them a sense of inclusion and importance.

But it did not always happen this way. Trips to Amul, and all that singing and chanting arranged by extension people, faded in the women's memory and they did not materially change in their relationship to the milk cooperatives. The Dudhsagar dairy in Mehsana, with its closer contact with grassroots communities, knew about the problem and wanted to do something, structurally, to anchor women into the milk cooperative institutions. For the organizers, an opportunity presented itself in the most unexpected manner. It was as follows.

Dudhsagar is one of the few milk cooperatives in India to put into practice the ideas to which everyone paid lip service. Dudhsagar wanted to do something basic in recognition of women's contributions. It therefore made women the co-members of grassroots bodies along with their husbands. The women of the district of Mehsana and, in particular, of Chaudhury caste, had already distinguished themselves as great breeders of animals. They literally established deep bonds between themselves and their animals, and coined a word for it, *athwar*; a word not found in the Gujarati (regional language) dictionary. When veterinary scientists wanted to see how their new experiments worked in the cowsheds, they often approached Chaudhury women. Those women proved to be equally keen on adopting the newly recommended practices in animal breeding. As a result, the veterinarians were full of praise for their rational understanding and speed in application.

Hence, when Dudhsagar decided to make women of Mehsana co-members of the village cooperative, along with their husbands, there were no protests on the part of either their husbands or from the people with unprogressive views. There was, in fact, quick acceptance of the decision in the district.

The co-membership of women, however, was not a celebration or recognition of women's contributions. It was, in fact, an attempt to get out of the sticky situation in which Dudhsagar had found itself. The men of the district, in search of better prices, had gone on strike in the late 1970s. They did not allow their women to go to the village cooperatives to pour milk, nor did they allow trucks to pick up the milk that was already collected in cans. For a day or two, the women did not know what to do. On the third day, they came in large numbers to Dudhsagar's headquarters in Mehsana city, and demanded an explanation from the top brass for the not picking up milk cans. The women's argument was that *they* were not on strike and that they were there to pour milk. This happened to break the strike that their men had launched. Simultaneously, the top brass also realized who their true allies were in the sprawling district of Mehsana. Soon after that, Dudhsagar introduced the scheme of co-membership for women, both as an insurance against men and also a reward for being true friends. Between husband and wife there was, however, one vote. But women were now co-recipients of loans as well as insurance on their animals.

The new status of women in the average village milk coopera-tive did not change things for them overnight. Initially, women went back to their daily chores. However, with an amount of extension work on the part of Dudhsagar, more and more women started coming in for deliberation and spent increasingly more time making their own arguments instead of coaching their men, as they had previously, on what to say in the meetings. Earlier, women's complaints had always been heard through a male voice. Now they were there to voice their own opinions. What these women were thus registering was an incremental pace of change in their gender as well as institutional relationships. The old ways of doing things were not completely rejected and, simultaneously, new practices were incorporated into the routine. There were, in fact, creeping extensions, imperceptible mixtures, and almost unnoticeable trans-formations taking place in those relationships.

Rural India, in its long history, has never seen any sudden or drastic social change, only deliberate change at a very gradual pace. Such a pace often disappoints the idealists and the restless, but it does give a sense of continuity to those whose lives have to go on in the old and recognizable ways while making diminutive room for the new.

Dudhsagar, through the proposed change, did not aim at an increased productivity in milk. There were other ways of doing this, namely, through more efficient animals, cattle feed, healthcare, and crossbreeding of animals. Through the co-membership of women, Dudhsagar created a counterweight to the wayward ways of men who were drawn into political ambition, which then vitiated the operative atmosphere of the grassroots institutions. Women, in that sense, were used in order to buy political peace in the district. And peace did prevail after their co-membership. Milk cooperatives, from then on, were treated as economic institutions strictly as means of livelihood and not as apparatus for ambitious politicians.

In the village of Irana, also within Dudhsagar's jurisdiction, women were used as troubleshooters. There, the men fought among themselves and failed their cooperative. Consequently, it was shut down for sometime and then restarted as a women's cooperative. We were there at the time of its reincarnation. The women had more than justified the trust its organizers placed in them. And what is more, Irana cooperative has now become a source of additional income for many families in the village.

Another byproduct of Dudhsagar's policy, albeit on a limited scale, is the emergence of women milk entrepreneurs in the district. Within the district now there are at least three women, Maltiben Chaudhury, Krishnaben Patel, and the younger sister of Krishnaben, who have extended the size of their herd by investing in good animals and by taking assistance from the extraordinary veterinary facilities provided by Dudhsagar. They sensed Dudhsagar's growing appreciation of their commitment to dairying. And that was correct. Those women were described and quoted in speeches by top officials of Dudhsagar as role models for other women to follow. These three women had gone beyond the counterweight role that was initially designed for them. Younger women in the district were so fascinated with these three women, that, before long, out of either emulation or envy, we might see more women entrepreneurs emerging in the district.

II. Women as Trained Co-Contributors

As the perception of women, held by various milk unions and the NDDB, has changed and evolved, so, too, has their participation in cooperative dairying. Women have plotted the course of this evolution instead of accepting pre-determined identity roles. The arrival of cooperative dairying at their doorstep, woke up rural women, as it were, to the various participatory and development opportunities that had opened up for them. Nothing like that had ever happened before. The women had now moved to the center of the milk unions' attention. Dairy officials from the various milk unions had been openly discussing their more extensive involvement.

On the part of the unions, the increase in productivity had to take precedence over the routine collecting, processing, and transporting of milk. One consideration important to productivity was the efficiency of the animals. Through proper feed, artificial insemination, and healthcare, the animals would be more productive. It also became important to properly train women who were at the center of milk economy. What could be done to help women become better managers of that economy? Could they be trained, by means of specially designed training programs, to perform their duties in a more effective manner?

Milk and milk products had always been a part of the Indian diet and celebratory consumption, but the target for the milk unions was to achieve collection, distribution, and delivery on a massive scale throughout that vast country by means of a milk grid, year round, through different seasons. And women had to be made aware of their importance in attaining this target. With this goal in mind, different unions had to come up with their own adaptations of training programs that were prepared by the NDDB. The idea was to prepare women for a more fruitful involvement in the milk cooperatives and not have them confined to merely cowshed activities.

Simultaneously, there was an attempt to identify potential leaders among the women and facilitate their development. Trained staff evaluated some of those programs. Let us now examine some of the efforts made by various milk unions and, later by the NDDB personnel, to train women to face additional responsibilities as co-

contributors, participants, decision-makers, leaders, and even as defenders of women's rights.

Earlier, most of the milk unions in their extension work had targeted women, to a lesser or greater degree, for training in dairying and participation in the working of cooperatives. Amul offered one of the earliest programs in that respect. In the mid-1980s, it was felt by Amul organizers that since women were more loyal and pliable than men, they ought not to be neglected and be given some recognition. Consequently, Amul recruited women extension workers to go to different villages and work under the supervision of its extension department. We attended some of those sessions and the following are our impressions of them.

Started as an attempt to seek a deeper involvement of women in various aspects of dairying, these extension programs to which women were exposed, in almost all the villages of the district, reminded them, "milk cooperatives belonged to their members and to no one else" (Somjee 1989:69). The idea was to embolden women into public participation and bring to the public forum the problems that they faced in various compartments of dairying. Implicit in this was an emphasis on recruiting the support of those who really mattered to dairying. Amul had recruited women extension workers with university degrees and ability to speak in Gujarati language. The extension workers told women not to be afraid of males and, in particular, those who occupied the dairy bureaucracy including the veterinarians. Ultimately, these men were their paid employees and were meant to serve the members of cooperatives. So in one fell swoop two dominant male images were demystified: men in the family, and men in the milk bureaucracy. No antagonistic expressions were used against males as such, only exhortations to female assertion in a range of activities related to dairying and the milk organization in general. The extension workers composed sentences for the female audience to complete with a collective chant. Songs were composed and collectively sung emphasizing the ownership of the milk cooperatives by members such as themselves.

It was a collective reaffirmation of proprietorship. In an earlier publication we described this: "The next stage was to help them acquire the culture of participation, by overcoming shyness and social constraints, and that by any standard was a Herculean task. By mid-1986, the (extension) instructors had covered as many as 868 villages of the district, covering a total of 117, 276 (women) milk producers" (Somjee 1989:73).

Women within the jurisdiction of Amul, in the district of Kheda, were thus exposed to the extension workers for a longer time than in other cooperatives. Consequently, they were some of the earliest to become *critical agents* within cooperative dairying.

The Cooperative Development Program

The NDDB made a concerted effort to give women members of the various milk unions training in what they called *cooperative development* and to encourage them to become leaders and voice their concerns. To this purpose the NDDB prepared a note in 1991 entitled *A Note on Cooperative Development* (NDDB 1991). In it, the NDDB encouraged women to participate in grassroots institutions. It outlined and prescribed what could be done to initially involve women in the cooperatives, and then identify and teach the requisite leadership skills. This two-pronged approach was significant because cooperative dairying was spreading to parts of India where the social and historical conditions did not support women-led cooperative undertakings. In addition, the NDDB acknowledged that resisting bureaucratic and political interference and preventing the mismanagement of funds by elected officials was a problem. What was necessary, therefore, was constant scrutiny of those in charge. The goal was to make everyone accountable. Finally, the NDDB explained that it was important to have a functional and effective relationship between the elected representatives and the professional managers within the organization (NDDB 1991).

A Note on Cooperative Development (NDDB 1991) also indicated a kind of rethinking on the part of the organizers of the NDDB who believed the "old style" education in cooperatives was not very helpful and that all sides involved in the successful functioning of the cooperatives should be made aware of their respective responsibilities. The NDDB seemed to recognize that the political world of Indian democracy had led to the degradation of various social and political institutions and wanted to prevent the same from happening in the milk cooperatives.

Let us now examine how the villages that were exposed to special programs for women's leadership fared. Here, various evaluative studies have presented different findings.

A report on Kheda district found that the program had heightened the awareness level of women (NDDB 1998:ii). Another report on the neighboring district of Mehsana presented similar findings. It maintained that the "Awareness level of women members has considerably improved in respect to some of the issues such as feeding, breeding, animal management, cleanliness and quality of milk" (Vijaya and Shankar Mohan 1998:v).

Both reports concluded that the program, in general, was far more important to women than to men. Moreover, in most milk unions at the district level, men welcomed the opportunity for their women to learn from such a program. The only exception to this was in Bihar and in Gujarat where men felt that they should control the cooperatives. They believed that men were as important to dairying as women. They argued that when animals had to be taken out for grazing, it was often men rather than women who performed those functions. These men thought that the organizations were focusing too closely on women, and that raising their level of importance would create problems in the long run. The farmers who expressed such views before us were essentially from the OBC communities of Bihar where respect for women as a social group was very low. Here, even the men had experienced disadvantage at the hands of higher castes, both economically and socially. Consequently, when the village-level milk cooperative arrived, a place where they had a voice and vote, they did not want to be marginalized once again, especially in relation to women. The men of Venkar caste (former untouchables) expressed a similar sentiment in Kheda district in the 1970s. They, too, did not want to face the question of whether dairying should increasingly become women's responsibility, even when it involved *their* women.

The attitude of the lower strata of men in general was as follows: Women had their own space where they could express themselves. Working at home, and looking after the family, in no way diminished them. For people of the lower social and economic strata, dairying was the joint responsibility of men and women. And it should, therefore, be kept that way. One of our respondents in a village in Bihar said "*sabaka man ak saman*" (everybody's dignity should be equally respected) and, therefore, why single out women for greater importance?

The NDDB's program for women's leadership in milk cooperatives was also not without its own problems. The NDDB's program was designed specifically to enable women to take over the *entire* range of dairy activity—not just in the cowshed, but also in the cooperative building where milk collection occurs, milk quality is tested, accounts are kept, meetings are held, and contacts with visiting dairy personnel from the union are maintained. The cooperatives run entirely by women did not face that problem, although it is natural that some of them would go further up the ladder. The problem arose in milk cooperatives with mixed membership where men ran the show as their divine right.

In the Kolhapur milk cooperatives, the arguments among men and women often became acrimonious. Men accused women of extracting special favors for themselves. Despite the bitterness, the work of the cooperatives remained unaffected. In economic terms, the Kolhapur union had done exceedingly well. It had significantly added to the already high income of the district from sugarcane. On top of that, the supply of buffalo milk to markets in Mumbai, at a high rate of return, had made the rural economy of the district a booming economy. But, according to some men, the extraordinary importance given to women seemed to be spinning out of control. Already women were on their way to getting a higher proportion of political representation, which was likely to be nearly one-third in the panchayat (local council), the state legislative assembly and, with some luck, in the *Lok Sabha* (Parliament). Women had also started entering the field of savings and loans, a field that, until then, was entirely managed by men. So, for many men, the leadership within the milk institutions was their "turf," and women were taking over with direct encouragement from the NDDB, or the *dairywallas*. Therefore, the dialogue concerning women's leadership was not always polite. By its very nature not only were the men going to be excluded from the leadership training, they were going to be replaced by women.

In Kolhapur, what often began as a jocular dialogue concerning who was most suited for leadership, often deteriorated into snide remarks about women's perceived inabilities and supposed "natural" limitations: "What do you want men to do? Sit at home like you?" asked a male member. A woman replied, "you are nothing but a *Pudhari*" (meaning "those who take you backwards" or the agents of regression). One thing seemed certain: women's ambition to "take over" the cooperatives was not going to be a straightforward process. It was going to play itself out against the background of gender relationships in the process of change in the wider society. While Bihar and Kolhapur did not envisage a smooth transfer of power to women, in some of the other states the transition was not that bad. In fact, in the tribal districts of Gujarat, where the gender distances are traditionally narrower, men applauded women and their march towards leadership roles.

Over and above the evaluations of women's leadership program, the NDDB also explored the possibility of a broader approach to women's empowerment through their increasing participation in cooperative dairying. The question was whether women's involvement in milk cooperative dairying, and in a wide range of activities related to it, could be used to accelerate the shrinking of gender distance itself?

Frances Sinha's study, entitled "Opportunities for Women's Empowerment through membership of Dairy Cooperative Societies" (Sinha 1999), identified the obstacles that faced the women's movement in cooperative dairying. After all, gender relations in any society do not operate in a vacuum. And in India the existing gender relations had been backed by historical, cultural, and religious factors. This had created a "social pattern" that was accepted and internalized by women. The author studied 50 milk cooperatives in Andhra Pradesh, Bihar, and Karnataka. She had come to the conclusion that despite exposure to the NDDB's programs, women had to struggle against their own limited literacy, a lack of confidence, and their habit of depending on men for most things.

V.M. Rao examined the involvement of women in dairying against the background of an NDDB report that claimed that "85% of India's national dairy husbandry activity (NDDB 1994a) are the responsibility of women" (Rao 1995:4). But such involvement did not register any dramatic shift in women's membership in cooperatives. It increased from 13.21 percent in 1960-1961 to 14.6 percent in 1993-1994. There was impressive growth, however, in the number of women who visited Amul: it increased from 14,151 in 1961-62 to 26,725 by 1993-94 (Rao 1995:23). The women-managed cooperatives distinguished themselves in another way: they collected more milk and had fewer disputes among their members.

One of the district milk unions, which made a systematic attempt to involve more women in dairying, was Kolhapur. In a sense, women experienced more disadvantage in the rural society of Kolhapur than expected, as it is located in the socially progressive state of Maharastra. Its feudal society and its continuing influence had made certain areas and jobs gender specific, most of which favored men. Consequently, women who wanted to get involved in various aspects of dairying were uncomfortable when there was a mixed situation. Women often became articulate and active when they were separated from men. Kolhapur, nevertheless, decided to give training to women in bookkeeping, correspondence, management, etc., along with a broad motivational training emphasizing the reasons it was important for them to get involved in areas other than the family cowshed.

Unlike the milk unions of Gujarat, Kolhapur did not ignore government servants who presided over the resources of the state. It, instead, motivated men and women to put their demands before them. But by and large, Kolhapur depended on the cohesion of women and built on that with the help of extension officers. Consequently, wherever women got involved, both in productivity and procurement, milk collection for the cooperative increased. That was often enough to silence the mocking men.

The social cohesion among the women of lower castes and, in particular, among the Dalits (former untouchables), was even higher. Under the guidance of an extension worker they became an efficient group ready to take on a variety of responsibilities. For them a new institutional status, with extensions worker guiding them on to new undertakings, also enhanced their sense of self-worth. Consequently, when questioned by a sympathetic extension worker, or even a visitor, they responded with some telling observations, often identifying the different problems that they faced and how, in their opinion, these problems could be solved. With Dr. Ambedkar's (India's greatest Dalit leader and the father of the Indian Constitution) picture hanging on the wall as inspiration, we questioned Dalit women, young and old, about their attitudes concerning the cooperatives. There seemed to be a consistent attitude among them: they did not want such a highly successful rural organization, such as the milk cooperative dairy, to be confined to milk only. They had a large number of social and economic problems and thought that the organization could do something about them. Given the opportunity to come together, with extension workers listening, they were even willing to discuss their family planning problems.

For its part, Kolhapur had woken up to the availability of a huge resource which it could now tap. The more these women succeeded, the more they inspired confidence in the union personnel of their involvement. In their case there were less politics, less hassle, an almost guaranteed increase in procurement, and compliance with the suggestions of the organizers. Naturally, the organizers welcomed such a positive response.

Social change in India, unlike in industrialized societies of the West, goes through a highly tortuous and incremental process. And while there is much to be said for encouraging change, there are also a lot of pitfalls in assuming that one can substitute Western feminist theories of adversarial relationships between men and women and the use of milk cooperatives to bring about such change overnight. Any program of reordering gender relationships in India, will have to take into account the basic cultural and historical premise that women, together with men, have done much to bring about an incremental change in gender relations (Somjee 1989).

Arun Wayagankar, in his study of Kolhapur women (1994), has argued that Gokul's (Kolhapur's) decision to "empower" women was very clear about one thing and that is milk cooperatives were simply an "entry point" for women from a society which was essentially based on patriarchy. The idea behind various extension programs was to convince women that they too can exercise control over the environment that surrounds them and improve their status. Once one becomes a decision-maker in dairying, one might want to play the same role in domestic situations. Consequently, the cooperative development program wanted to strengthen the participatory position of women in cooperatives first, and then take the advantage of her cooperative "empowerment" to increase her influence in the family (Wyangankar 1994).

The NDDB women's empowerment program is considered one of the largest in the world. Wayangankar explains, "Approximately 2,500 village-level dairy cooperatives are covered by the CD program each year, with 250,000 rural women trained annually.

These women are made aware of their rights and roles in their cooperatives, thus initiating their empowerment process" (Wayangakar 1994).

Viji Srinivasan, one of the dedicated social activists among women who has spent a major part of her professional life in grassroots communities, has argued that right across the full range of cooperatives there is a lot of enthusiasm and positive feelings on the part of women who are running them. Perhaps, if there is one institution that they can call their own, it is the village-level milk cooperative (Srinivasan 1986).

III. Women as Critical Agents

So far we have examined how women were first treated as targets and then as conduits by the milk unions to achieve some of their goals. They were viewed as a useful resource for the dairy industry and therefore were trained by means of extension work and specifically designed cooperative development programs. In this section, we will examine instances when women, either on their own initiative or as a result of the extension work, turned into *critical agents* within the broad framework of milk cooperatives. In their demands they often went beyond what the organizers of milk unions expected. In some cases, they succeeded in getting favorable responses, but in others only a few polite words indicating an inability to act or indifference. The extraordinary thing about this is that women's demands came from states that were at the top of dairy industry such as Gujarat, at one end, as well as states like Rajasthan and Bihar, where the milk cooperatives had yet to make their mark, at the other. In this section we shall examine a variety of such demands which women as critical agents made on their dairy organizers.

Amul Women's Demand for Family Healthcare

Over the years, Amul Dairy kept up its extension work among the women of Kheda district. One of the themes that the extension workers repeatedly touched upon was the importance of animal healthcare. They often tried to convey the basic principle of dairying: the greater the healthcare and hygiene of animals, the greater the productivity. This was repeatedly emphasized. Moreover, the highly efficient animal healthcare system introduced by Amul, resulting in enhanced milk productivity, was there for everyone to see. Even in the late 1960s when Amul dairy had been in existence for over two decades, its veterinary units boasted that they could provide emergency help within four hours to any village in the district. Consequnetly, the villagers were full of admiration and gratitude.

The admired healthcare system for the animals, however, did not have a human counterpart. The villagers, in particular the women, pointed this out again and again. The women would complain, "when my animal falls ill, it receives veterinary care in less than four hours; but when my child falls ill, there is no such help even when he/she is close to death." Such remarks were uttered, time and again in front of deeply embarrassed veterinarians.

Groups of women from various villages, untutored by extension workers, repeatedly went to Amul Dairy's top managers requesting the organization for a healthcare system for their families, and were told again and again: "We are only *dudhwallas* [dairymen]! We can look after your animals. For your children you have to go to state-run health units." And whenever women replied that such units existed in name only, the organizers would merely shrug their shoulders. Nevertheless, over the years, these women from different villages kept up the pressure. Finally, the top brass of Amul Dairy relented and began looking for a workable solution to this difficult problem. After examining various proposals for training village women for a few years, Amul Dairy finally decided, in 1980, to implement a health linkage. The proposal was to train two women at the village level as health workers who would attend to minor illnesses. They would remain in touch with two trained roving nurses in the district for guidance in complicated cases. And finally, the nurses themselves would be in touch with doctors at the headquarters or with the nearby Krishna Hospital for further help. That hospital, in recent years, has made a great name for itself for the high quality health service that it provides to the region.

The initial funding for this proposal came from the purse given to one of the founding fathers of Amul, namely, Tribhuvandas K. Patel (TK), when he retired after four decades of distinguished service. He gave the entire amount to what came to be known as the Tribhuvandas Foundation (TF). Then there were financial donations from Amul Dairy itself, as well as from UNICEF, the British Overseas Ministry, and others. The scheme initially charged a nominal amount of Rs.10, but now it has been raised to Rs.25 (U.S.$0.55) a year for all members of the cooperative. And, Amul Dairy, willingly or unwillingly, has continued to underwrite the remaining expenses every year. As more and more villages were brought under the scheme, the bill for Amul Dairy also increased. By the year 2000, it was roughly Rs.4 crores (US$888,888) a year.

The TF also succeeded in attracting the services of Dr. Uma Vyas, a successful medical practitioner of Indian origin, in London, wanting to return home and to serve her people. She built a world-class, rural based medical system.[3]

Vyas and her associates undertook the difficult task of building a medical team, which would have credibility not only with the skeptical villagers, but also with the state health units that thought the TF was trespassing on their turf. In 20 years since its inception, it has covered more than 638 villages in the district. As a rule, it avoided big villages where district medical services, operated by the state, were available in one form or another. One of the unexpected tasks the Foundation was required to perform related to family planning. Women in grassroots communities had known "Umaben," (Dr. Uma Vyas) during her many visits to their villages and wanted *her* to look after them at the Foundation's headquarters. While this was a tribute to her, it, nevertheless, vastly increased her responsibilities.

So, what started off as a demand of grassroots women in milk cooperatives for their families, as they acted as critical agents in a complex chain of events, ended up providing a health service for rural people. Nothing, however, would have come out of such a demand had it not been for Amul's economic muscle, Kurien's vision, and Vyas's organizational ability and dedication to translate an initial proposal into a living rural reality. On the downside, the Foundation's healthcare bill, which was Amul's responsibility, led to the pronouncement that such a health scheme was not replicable elsewhere. In reality, given Amul's earnings, the amount needed for such a health scheme was close to one percent. The same would have been true for the other premier dairies of Gujarat had they decided to have a similar healthcare system. But they did not. In cooperative dairy circles, however, this issue is not dead. Another round of demands by women as critical agents, elsewhere, might bring it back to the center cooperatives' attention.

Bihar: The Use of Female Catalyst

Let us now turn from India's most prosperous state, Gujarat, to the least prosperous, namely, Bihar. Despite great political instability, economic backwardness, inequitable distribution of land, and an indifferent bureaucracy, the women of Bihar villages, where cooperatives had struck roots, gave an extraordinary account of themselves.

While the urban scene in Bihar has been depressing, mercifully, the rural communities in its districts such as Vaishali, Samastipur, and near Patna, close to the holy river Ganges, enjoyed agricultural prosperity. The bulk of the milk cooperatives there depended on buffalo as the primary source of milk. The buffalo had been the animal of the lower strata of rural society almost all over India, as they do not require as much investment as do the crossbred (CB) cows. Besides, Bihar is not as familiar with CB economics (i.e., greater productivity, early lactation, and above all greater yield in summer months when the price of milk rises), as are the more experienced dairying states of India. Nevertheless, the emulative milk producers in search of higher returns have gradually started switching over to crossbred cows.

Yadav women seemed to be playing a role similar to the Chaudhury women in Mehsana district in Gujarat in the switch to crossbred cows. Most of the Bihari villages started off with a few buffalo. Then when veterinarians got involved in helping milk producers to buy CBs, especially when animal traders came from Punjab and Haryana, women went with their men to select the animals. Women successfully managed a number of milk cooperatives in various districts of Bihar, regardless of their overall backwardness and illiteracy. Despite being latecomers, Bihar's women-run cooperatives have done well. The only assurance their men needed was that such cooperatives would remain unmixed in terms of gender.

The women in such villages went far beyond the routine management of milk collection, milk testing, can-filling, ledger writing, and making payments. Surprisingly enough, in some of these villages, women, after initial training, also became lay inseminators of animals. That, however, did not happen very often, even in Gujarat despite its veteran status in dairying. Rarely did women of Gujarat agree to be trained as lay inseminators. Even after training, one was not sure how long they would stick to their newly acquired profession. In Bihar, on the other hand, Rajput, Yadav, and Koeri girls, with encouragement from their fathers and husbands, began coming into the insemination profession. In some cases, their fathers and husbands were either doctors or professionals. This class of Bihar's rural population always encouraged its female children to go into technical fields within dairying. Such an attraction would not have been there had the veterinary services not been accorded the status, mystique, and caring image of the medical profession itself.

For the management of all aspects of dairying, therefore, the state of Bihar, despite its many shortcomings, suddenly discovered a new resource: its women. But there was more to it than that. Men discovered that when women managed those cooperatives, there was less politics. This was welcome in a state where politics had sunk to the level of ignoring the public good altogether. The women now had an organization of their own, and they wanted to show both their men and the dairy organizers that they also mattered.

Development scholars, in recent years, had coined a pejorative label for Bihar, and that is: *bimaru,* or "sick state." This was true of Bihar despite that it has nearly 40 percent of India's mineral resources, some of its most fertile agricultural lands, and an abundance of water supply in most of its districts. The question then was whether the arrival of its women would make a difference? Once women become a part of the work force there is the possibility of a chain reaction, as was shown in states such as Kerala, Karnataka, Andhra Pradesh, Tamil Nadu, etc. In some of the districts of those states, as Nobel laureate Amartya Sen has pointed out, even the birthrate has started falling, bringing it to a level similar to China, without its accompanying brutality (Sen 1995). Time alone will tell whether what Bihar is doing now, namely, bringing in women to the forefront, is enough to overcome its lost development time.

Rajasthan: Women Demand a Comprehensive Approach

The milk cooperatives of Rajasthan, as we saw earlier, had a troubled beginning. This is because its bureaucrats jealously guarded an independent approach to dairying which they themselves had proposed. On the positive side, however, they did want women to play a more active role in dairying.

Despite several impediments, in terms of literacy and health, the women of Rajasthan were constantly exploring a comprehensive role for the dairy organizations. Although the literacy rate among its women had doubled in the last ten years (it was 44 percent in 2001), their understanding of the problem of health and hygiene had remained limited. Such limitations notwithstanding, its women drew attention to problems in areas other than milk for which they wanted a cooperative solution. In the meetings that we attended, women always pressed the organizers to provide a cooperative marketing solution for their agricultural crops such as tomatoes, peas, and grains. They argued, unsuccessfully, that milk was a much smaller proportion of their agricultural crop. They kept on pressing for the establishment of parallel cooperatives for their agricultural products and the organizers continued to give them evasive answers. Evidently, there was a dearth of social activists in the region to take up the proposal for cooperatives for agricultural products and then put pressure on the organizers.

In a sense, the women of Rajasthan had surprised the milk bureaucracy by fulfilling their targets (for milk, literacy, income generating schemes, etc.) in the shortest possible time, and then turning around and telling them to build parallel cooperatives for marketing their agricultural products. As women saw it, there was more potential there than in milk. They were disappointed when men from Jaipur, where the cooperative headquarters were located, did not want to discuss this. In the feudal society of rural Rajasthan, men now appeared to be losing the upper hand, which their traditional thinking had mistakenly told them that they would always have. They had to listen to women for new ideas that might have great possibilities. While the women did not get their lateral cooperatives, their increased participation in the local dairy activity and the economy enhanced their confidence and self-esteem.

Andhra Pradesh: Women Defend Milk Cooperative

The Ford Foundation, with the help of the NDDB, had initially established 102 women's cooperatives in the Chittoor district of Andhra Pradesh (Sen and Rhani 1990:809-831). Over the years, some of them did not do very well. Out of those that survived, we studied seven. One criterion that guided our selection was their survivability in the face of a private dairy called, *The Heritage Dairy*, which had been launched and sustained by state politicians.

Unfortunately, there were few laws to prevent conflicts of interest in India, and those that did exist were hardly put to the test in court. Consequently, politicians were able to undermine the milk cooperatives of Chittoor, which had been started with great idealism and assiduously sustained by its women. In these cooperatives, women showed extraordinary resistance in not yielding to the direct and indirect pressure exerted by politicians. The women who resisted the dissolution of milk cooperatives were also, in most cases, their founding members. They, therefore, had a protective interest in them. The politicians tried to hide behind India's new policy of liberalization, which was supposed to introduce competition and serve the consumer better. They did not want to answer the women who accused them of using the resources of their office to make that competition unfair. The milk cooperatives were not able to get loans from the district's financial institutions, some of them cooperative banks themselves, because the politicians in power exerted pressure on them.

Furthermore, in almost all the milk cooperatives in Chittoor district, the organizers were pressured to keep the politicians' milk cans. Hence, in village after village one could see the green cans of the *Heritage Dairy* side-by-side with the usual aluminum cans of milk cooperatives. Of special interest to us was the background of the women and the rationale they offered for protecting their institutions. The two agriculturist castes, which were involved in dairying, were the Kammas and the Reddys. Their women, along with women of backward and scheduled castes had, in most cases, a secondary level education. Moreover, women with more education, some of them schoolteachers or wives of professional people, were also deeply involved in milk cooperatives. While all these women were firmly anchored in traditional, religious, and family values, they had also absorbed democratic ideals. They believed that women should speak for themselves in defense of their rights and institutions.

The politicians of the state, therefore, had quite a fight on their hands. They were fighting women who were inspired by a time-honored ideal of fighting for what they held dear. Some of these women were also veterans of the fight against liquor consumption, which resulted in the closure of a number of liquor shops (Stackhouse 1993). Besides, the politicians themselves were not sure of what kind of political fallout of a more drastic approach would entail. So, they had decided to go the "competition" route, which they were confident would eventually wear down those "cooperative-crazy," grassroots women. Given the resources of the politicians, they were in no hurry to do anything as drastic as taking over the cooperatives for the non-payment of money or "financial mismanagement," the two usual reasons for seizure. The women feared such a possibility and were also preparing to go to court to defend their institutions. We also witnessed a *dharna* (sit down strike) staged on the grounds of the dairy by these militant women.

Everyone was treading cautiously in what had become a political minefield, not only for union officials, but also for politicians. For the women who stood by the milk cooperatives, it was not only something they had built, it was also an institution that embodied their ideals and, therefore, was worth fighting for. Moreover, those cooperative institutions, in village after village, had become the centers of community activity. Ever since their establishment, the local panchayats, where men were interminably squabbling, had faded into the background. Furthermore, through the cooperatives and the union in Chittoor, these villages sent pure milk and *ghee* (clarified butter) to the highly revered Tirupati temple in the neighborhood. The cooperatives had assured a steady supply of quality milk and milk products to the temple. In serving it, these deeply religious villages of the south also felt that they had enjoyed the protection and blessings of the deity that presided over the temple. Thus, those women were not only involved in helping themselves economically, but were also serving a cause higher than their livelihood.

In the villages where there were mixed gender cooperatives, the men showed muted resentment to what the politicians were doing.

They were resigned to the thought that the politicians, given their hold on power and resources, will ultimately win out. They therefore often used to encourage those milk producers, who routinely brought poor quality milk, to pour it in the milk cans belonging to politicians for which there were fewer tests and lower payments. Such cans are easily identified by their green color. Milk contained in such cans, as stated earlier, did not fetch a good price in the market.

In contrast to the women, the men had adopted a policy of live and let live and told themselves that it was wise to be practical, especially in this world where nothing lasts for ever, much less a bunch of powerful politicians. And they were proved right. The politicians who promoted the private dairy did not do well in the state assembly election of 2004. In fact they were unexpectedly thrown out of office. The question was: what role did the women supporting milk cooperatives play in the political downturn of such politicians? It is too early to tell.

The Ford Foundation had also taken a special interest in women's cooperatives in Chittoor. One of their findings was that educating women about the functioning of dairies and the role they could play in them would go a long way in making a difference to their situation (Samakhaya n.d.).

Tamil Nadu: Women as Critics of the Milk Bureaucracy

One of the districts in India that should have done better in terms of its milk cooperatives is Erode in Tamil Nadu. Erode had some of the finest milch animals in the country and had milk cooperatives as far back as the 1930s. However, the politicians in Chennai (Madras) interfered with milk prices. The politicians had interfered with the market mechanism that normally determines the price of milk in other parts of India. But what was most disheartening to the milk producers was that even the state judiciary had failed to protect the autonomy of the milk cooperatives.

While the traders collected the bluk of milk in the district, the SCs and the OBCs had hung on to their milk cooperatives hoping that some day they will give a good fight to the politicians in power by supporting their rivals during elections. That has always remained a possibility in Tamil Nadu where there are frequent changes in the fortunes of political parties. More impatient on this count are the women in milk cooperatives. They think that the bureaucrats in various milk unions, who shy away from fighting for the interests of cooperatives, are equally to be blamed.

This anger on the part of the women in milk cooperatives was particularly evident in a village, now an emerging town, called Nasianur. It is on the outskirts of the city of Erode and women run the cooperative. Situated on a crossroad of highways, Nasianur did extremely well by selling a portion of its milk collection locally. It charged a higher price to its local customers. The township had numerous shops selling sweets and tea stalls, and, as a result, it needed good quality milk; the milk was supplied by the Nasianur cooperative. Among its regular customers were a number of educational institutions, and some cooperative members were alumni of those institutions.

The women of Nasianur were considered to be very progressive. For instance they had succeeded in restricting the size of their families. The village even boasted of having attained the prestigious status of a "one-child village," but admitted privately to us that that was the case with only 60 percent of its population. The remaining 40 percent had two children at the most. The women had put up billboards on all roads entering the city saying that it was a one-child village. Some of their milk vans also had such advertisements painted on them. Apparently, women had put their education to good use. Their rationale for having one-child, boy or girl, was that it would be the most effective way to provide care and give the child the best developmental opportunities. They felt the government could not be trusted to provide those opportunities. As they were educated mothers themselves, they saw no difficulty in women having the same opportunity as men. As a result, they felt that it was fine to have a girl as the only child in the family.

Since they had fought their way through social inhibitions and taboos, the women of Nasianur were troubled by the unwillingness of the Erode Union bureaucracy to fight the politicians of the state. After all, every few years the politicians came begging for votes, so the women believed the Erode Union should have organized the local farmers in order to teach the politicians a lesson at the polls. They even argued that the Union should not have gone to court. The court takes years to give a decision and there is no guarantee of the outcome. So why not settle it at the polls? Nasianur women thus spoke with a political savvy rarely seen in rural India. Their education and peri-urban location, and encounters with men while managing the cooperative, had emboldened them. In the winter of 2000, the question was whether or not their anger would have an electoral impact.

Valsad: Incredible Response from Tribal Women

Vasudhara in Valsad, as we saw earlier, had a remarkable success in inducting tribal women into the milk economy. Most of them who took to dairying had been *majoors* (laborers), who remembered with gratitude where they had come from and what the cooperatives had done for them. Women ran more than 60 percent of Valsad's cooperatives. Cooperative dairying had not only made a difference to their standard of living, but also provided them and their family with the means for further economic and educational development. In such advancements, the tribal women had played a crucial role.

Since the traditional gender distance between men and women in tribal society is more narrower than the one in society with castes, almost effortlessly Sumul and Valsad were able to have a large number of women as chairwomen in their cooperatives (Somjee 1989:145-149).

In the early 1990s, Sumul organizers told us that tribal women, and for that matter women of any background, had difficulty in managing bookkeeping and other responsibilities. However, by the year 2000 that view had changed. Now the tribal women even visit the offices of Sumul in Surat city, and Vasudhara in Valsad city, to discuss some additional activities they plan to undertake. The union executives welcomed such a change. Valsad's social activist managing director, Vashibhai, explained his position to us: "If women can be brought into dairying you can trigger off a number of development processes in rural India which will have far reaching consequences. They are a major development resource and they can change the rural scene. What you need is a vision to bring them on board and highly pragmatic schemes which can bear quick result and continue their interest in what they are doing."

Vashibhai thus wanted to use tribal women within the framework of cooperative dairying as a *trigger* to activate a chain reaction that would go beyond milk. He wanted to involve them in projects relating to health and hygiene, education, biogas, and micro saving. He firmly believed that the tribal women would be able to influence women in other social groups. For him, tribal women in a cooperative situation had the potential to bring about social change in rural India.

Vashibhai the visionary was also a highly practical person. The more he pondered over the human resources of the district, consisting largely of the tribals, the more he felt challenged to do something unique for the district. Already the neighboring district of Surat had proved that the adivasis could be brought into cooperative dairying provided one had a socially concerned staff willing to work with them. But that was not enough for Vashibhai. He wanted to go beyond Sumul, focus on the adivasi women, put them in charge of dairying, and set the men free to do something else.

Initially, the local banks were indifferent to his proposal of giving tribal women loans. He approached the board of Vasudhara union and asked them to become involved. In less than two years after taking loans from Vasudhara, the tribal women, with the help of their high milk yielding animals, not only returned the entire amount of the loans, but also started receiving a sizable amount to cover family expenses. After spending money on agriculture, stainless steel utensils, the improvement of dwellings, TVs, VCRs, etc., tribal women began to wonder what should be done with their surplus income. The local banks asked them, respectfully, to deposit their money in the banks with various kinds of high interest yielding schemes. Initially, they welcomed the advice of the banks. Some of the villages in the district that had a population of OBCs along with the tribals, registered a monthly income between Rs.4,000 to 12,000 (U.S.$88.88 to $266.66 per household).[4] For the first time ever, the tribal women of India had money to spare and, possibly, to invest.

Social activists on Vasudhara's staff were asked to pay special attention to the emerging problem of savings. The staff was told to advise, and not "lead" the tribal women, in their saving and investing activities. The idea being that at some stage they must learn how to invest their savings on their own. Following their advice, the women decided to form their own saving and lending groups. It was up to them to select groups with which they were most comfortable. Most groups comprised of approximately 20 members. The amount that they contributed each month differed from group to group and village to village. Generally, investments ranged from Rs.20 to Rs.100 (U.S.$0.41 to $2.22) per month. A village called Railia Falia had the highest rate of investment, from Rs.100 to Rs.500 (U.S.$2.22 to $11.11) per family each month. Such savings groups were known as women's self-help groups. The money was initially kept in the bank to earn interest. But if a member or her relative wanted a loan, the interest charged was usually about 2 percent per month, 24 percent annually. Since banks did not consider any applications for loans from them, and the money lenders asked for more than 33 percent per annum, loans from the women's saving groups were the cheapest. Rarely was money borrowed for more than three months, and rate of repayment was very quick.

Not all self-help groups were lending groups. Money was collected in a group and deposited in the bank. Given the rural banks' reputation for unhelpfulness, the average tribal woman was happy to save collectively and watch the savings and interest grow month by month in her account in the group's bankbook. In a span a few years, several savings groups were formed in the district. And every member of these groups was pleased to see her savings (with interest) grow month after month.

We looked at this micro-savings phenomenon in three different villages of the district: Gohlar, Pratapnagar, and Railia Falia. The first two were tribal women's cooperatives and the last was a tribal cum OBC women's cooperative.

The Gohlar cooperative was established in 1993. Its income from milk was Rs.3.7 lakhs (U.S.$8,222). Six years later, in 1999, it jumped to Rs.17 lakhs (U.S.$37,777). This was largely due to the introduction of crossbred cows. Consequently, the women now had more money to save.

The Pratapnagar tribal women were more educated. Their savings group also had large amounts to invest. And they did not hesitate when it came to lending to start business in a nearby town. All the borrowers, even when the money was used for commercial undertakings, repaid their debt in about a year and half.

Finally, the most ambitious group of women was in Railia Falia. It had a large number of saving groups. Even its high school children saved their pocket money, deposited it collectively in the local bank, and had it earn interest.

Saving had thus become a kind of a habit for the villagers. The women of Railia Falia wanted a Mahila (women's) Bank to be started in the district by bringing together all the saving groups. They estimated that the women of an average village saved Rs.2 lakhs (U.S.$4,444) annually, and with a close to thousand villages in the district, that added up to about Rs.2 crores (U.S.$444,444) per year. And if Vasudhara Dairy deposited an equivalent amount, and so did Gujarat government, the Mahila Bank would have Rs.6 crore (1.33m) plus interest coming in every year. This would make quite a respectable little bank of their own and would do away with the hassle that they faced when dealing with a scheduled bank. The women of Railiafalia, however, stipulated that the scheme should be called the "Valsad Pattern of Women's Savings Bank."

The tribal women of Valsad thus did not stop at milk or milk cooperative. They, with the help of social activists of the region, went beyond it. They already had entered the field of micro-saving and lending. And, they wanted to keep going as long as they received help and encouragement from social activists. In a list of comparative membership and savings, on the part of self-help groups in 55 milk unions across the country, the women of Valsad ranked as one of the top few.

IV. Self-Involvement and Ethnodevelopment

The preceding sections suggest that the milk cooperatives had a variety of goals and perspectives when they decided to involve women as leaders. In this section, we shall briefly reconsider them and also consider whether women's involvement in those functions helped them grow in their social and political capacity or not. One thing is certain: cooperatives, for their own reasons, brought their institutions to the doorstep of women, and gave them the opportunity to get involved in a variety of new roles and functions. Such involvement, as we shall argue in this section, benefited the women. Their involvement in each new function assigned to them helped them grow in their capacities. By participating in decision-making processes, discussing their problems with visiting veterinarians, and organizing micro-saving and lending activities, the women of those villages gained self-confidence and came to realize their potential. Through these processes they became full-fledged participants in their grassroots organizations and took their first steps towards becoming active members of society.

The thinking of the organizers, initially, was not clear on what roles women in cooperative dairying should play. As women performed effectively in each new role assigned to them, the organizers' respect for their abilities grew. Their initial approach of *using* women to boost milk productivity gave way to treating them as a new resource for specific purposes.

Simultaneously, the involvement of women in new roles and functions enhanced their social and political capacity, or what we have elsewhere called, *ethnodevelopment* (G. Somjee 1989; A.H. Somjee 1982). Their participation in the milk cooperatives increased their sense of self-worth and they could no longer be ignored.

For their part, the milk union organizers came to recognize that, despite their gender, women could perform, individually and jointly, important tasks in the development process that served everyone. That gender difference merely made certain tasks gender specific without the element of hierarchy in their relative importance. The evolution of cooperative dairying in India thus became, for women, a vast school for learning and exploring their talents over and above the traditional roles and functions assigned to them by society. The more they engaged themselves in cooperative dairying, the more they surprised themselves and the dairy organizers.

For a long time, dairying was considered to be another family or household task, like housekeeping or cooking, ideally suited to women. It took some time to realize that there was more to dairying than just household chores and that women would be taking on major responsibility in looking after them. On their part, the women found a unique opportunity that literally came to their doorstep to involve them in a set of closely-knit activities. As human beings who were traditionally consigned to a secondary position in all fields, the women empowered themselves through their participation in the many facets of the dairy industry. For a long time women had even internalized a view of themselves as being less important to their family and society. They, therefore, needed opportunities to involve themselves in processes that could bring them out of that sense of marginality. And those opportunities were provided by milk cooperatives at the grassroots level.

Such an involvement helped build their new persona. It not only helped them grow in their social and political capacity, but also enter a world beyond the confines of the family to that of their neighborhood and community. Their transformation from family-bound individuals to community individuals happened with considerable ease. Barring some issues such as health, they did not even have to agitate for more opportunities.

Depending on where they stood in the social hierarchy, women's involvement enabled them to rid themselves of various antecedent disadvantages. For upper caste women, talking to male strangers was a taboo. But those who participated in cooperative institutions gradually overcame that disadvantage. At the other end of the social spectrum, tribal women, with much less gender distance, overcame the disadvantage of their lack of knowledge concerning financial matters when they became members of the micro-saving groups in their community. In a real sense, therefore, the dairy revolution in India truly benefitted not only the rural poor but also women.

One could thus chart, *post facto,* the phases of ethnodevelopment of women as they got involved in the various sequences of dairying activity. The following sections identify and describe these phases.

Entering the Occupation of Dairying

Switching to dairying from other means of livelihood, including working in the fields of big landowners or roadside construction, was a big step forward for most women in the tribal group. We interviewed several tribal women in their late twenties and early thirties, who were involved in that kind of backbreaking toil. They had bitter memories of the work they had to do, and the inhumane treatment that they received at the hands of supervisors and contractors. The bulk of women in that age group were the veterans of *majoori* and they were also the people who told us how their lives had changed. They could now afford to keep their children in school longer. Also, they were able to meet expenses for food, improvements of dwelling, transportation, and so on. For such women, then, their very involvement in dairying became an enabling process. It enabled them to be free from physical drudgery and provided them with a better income for themselves and their families.

Enhanced Institutional Status

As discussed earlier, many women in rural India had been involved in dairying for generations. For example, the Chaudhury women of Mehsana had become expert breeders of milch animals. They and their families had enjoyed the ever-increasing income from the family cowsheds. What really transformed the lives of Chaudhury women along with others, however, was Dudhsagr Dairy's decision to make them co- members of milk cooperatives along with their husbands. Thereafter they made steady progress with regard to public involvement and decision-making. After that, one could see a gradual progress in their public involvement concerning important decisions. There was a time when they used to tutor their husbands on what to say in public meetings. Then they started accompanying them, occasionally correcting them, taking over from them, and then making forceful presentations on their own. So women who once spoke through a male voice now acquired a voice of their own. Their co-membership emboldened them to say their piece in public meetings whenever they thought it was necessary. They respected elders and men of their husbands' age group by means of *laaj* (women cover their faces before male elders as a mark of respect), and yet insisted on saying their piece, even in their presence.

While in a large number of villages many women either did not attend meetings, or attended but did not speak, they certainly bene-fited considerably by various cooperative development programs examined in this chapter. Such women needed more education and help, given the traditional nature of the rural society that inhibited them.

From Animal Healthcare to Human Healthcare

Animal healthcare, which dairy organizations provided, changed the perception of women in the cowshed. The women made a connection between animal healthcare and services for human health. While animal healthcare was provided by the cooperative organization, they had to agitate and demand (as we saw earlier in Amul's villages) for human healthcare. And they succeeded in getting a favorable response. As a result of their demand, and with help of Amul, the Tribhuvandas Fourndation put in place India's finest rural health service. The Foundation, by the year 2000-2001, had covered nearly 638 villages and had yet to cover the remaining one-third villages in the district (Tribhuvandas Fourndation 2000:3). Persuading other cooperatives to put in place similar health schemes in their respective districts proved much more difficult.

The demand for a human healthcare network was, in a sense, a natural evolution in the health attitudes of women, from their animals to their family. The women who managed the family cowsheds along with the veterinarians got involved in a joint process of delivering animal healthcare. Once this was fully operational, it was just a matter of time before they turned their thoughts from animals to human healthcare.

Partners in Improving Productivity

In Dudhsagar, the impact of research-minded veterinarians—who involved women in their drive to look after not only the health of the animal but also breed more efficient animals—was different from other regions. There, the women became the research arms of veterinarians, and the result was that, despite their limited literacy, they became well informed on questions relating to animal health-care and improvement in animal breed. The *vet-women* linkage in Mehsana resulted in an enormous improvement in the quality of dairy animals. Mehsana thus owes its status as a *mega* milk cooperative of India and Asia to its women and the veterinarians who involved them in their drive to improve the milch animal.

The women of Mehsana also wanted to go from animal health to human health. Toward this objective, various discussions took place but did not bear fruit. The excuse of the top brass was that it would cost too much money. Given Mehsana's finances in the year 2000, such an excuse was neither believed nor accepted. While the Tribhuvandas Foundation costs 1 percent of Amul's total income from milk for its health services, a corresponding health service would have cost not more than 0.6 percent of the revenue of Mehsana. The women of Mehsana deserved such a provision in recognition of their contributions to the district's economy.

Involvement in Micro Savings and Lending

Nothing stimulated the involvement of women more than the saving and lending activity in their village. And all this happened to tribal women who until a few years ago had to do *majoori* to provide food for their family! The income from milk in the newly established women's cooperatives, as we saw in this chapter, put most women in the category of potential savers and lenders. Initially they spent their newly acquired income on additional food and clothing for the family, and after that on urgent repairs or improvements to their dwellings. Subsequently, the social activists from Vasudhara Dairy targeted them for saving and lending plans. In the beginning, the majority of these women did not believe that they could save, let alone lend. Then came the formation of women's saving groups under the supervision of the social activists. The amount to save each month was decided by means of discussion among all the women members present in the group. Soon those members realized that it was not difficult for them to put away a small amount each month. And as their savings grew, along with added income from interest, so did their self-confidence. They realized they could not only earn enough, but also save. Then came the proposal that they could borrow from these groups or even lend money to an outsider provided they scrutinized the plan for the borrowed money. Such an exercise built women's capacity for handling money: from saving, to calculating the income from savings, to lending for specific purposes, to organizing repayment of the principal with interest.

After the meetings of the saving and lending groups, one could notice an air of added self-confidence and security among the women. In our presence, one of the group quoted a Gujarati saying: "*pin kame to pet bharaye, pun dhan kame to dhagala thai*" or "if we earn ourselves, at the most we can feed ourselves. But if our money earns more money for us, then we shall have a bundle of it!"

Of all the activities in which women of various milk cooperatives got involved, no other activity built their social and economic capacity more than the financial transactions of saving, lending, earning, and reinvesting. Income, health, education of their children, etc., were all very important, but they did not build women's self-worth as much as the transactions where money was involved. For those who were economically deprived for so long, it was a material as well as psychological experience of great significance. However, at that stage of their development, these women could not have done it on their own. They needed the social activists to bring them together, set up new economic goals, encourage them when they felt dejected, and tell them at every step that more could be achieved through effort.

The women of Chittoor district in Andhra Pradesh, or the women of Erode district in Tamil Nadu, gained in their political capacity as they involved themselves in openly criticizing how milk cooperatives in their respective milk unions were managed. For them, the milk cooperatives had become a kind of a school for learning and practicing how to participate effectively in the public domain.

In building women's social and political capacity, social activists had no doubt played an important part. But equally important was the role of men, either as fathers, brothers, husbands, or sons, who stood by their women in the process of their development. Women's development was also a matter of pride for the rest of the family including the males.

The women who involved themselves in the various processes of milk cooperative dairying were also persons with their own families, with men in them. And as they grew in stature and importance to their community, the men close to them benefited from their progress. Often the men celebrated the advancement of the women. Successful women, like successful men, brought credit to the family. Women occupied a new domain that was available to either men or women. And if the milk bureaucracy favored women in such common domains, the women could not be blamed. When such domains became gender specific, favoring women, men moved to other unoccupied or self-created domains. Consequently, the rise and success of women, with rare exceptions, did not lead to gender conflicts. In short, the cooperative dairies of India had provided a rare opportunity for women to grow through their involvement in sequestered domains where they did not incur the wrath of men.

Chapter 4

Participation and Human Development

Human development, as one of the major components of social and economic advancement, is not a new concept. While all major religions and social philosophies have emphasized its importance, by and large they have left it to individuals to pursue it through inquiry into the meaning and purpose of life. With the growth of political liberalism—as shaped by the ideas of Aristotle, John Locke, John Stuart Mill, Montesquieu, Emmanuel Kant, Thomas Jefferson, John Dewey, John Rawls, and others, the concept of human development came to acquire institutional and participatory dimensions. With these thinkers, human development was no longer a private pursuit, but one that required institutional provisions to facilitate participation in public policy decisions that govern the community. Among liberal thinkers, John Dewey put an extraordinary emphasis on participation as a means to develop human potential. He believed that a participant individual had a greater possibility of growing in his/her individual and social capacity than those who did not have such facilities.

Within the social sciences, economists were the last to discover the importance of human development to social and economic advancement. They had restricted their attention to economic growth and distribution, and only recently included education, health, the environment, quality of life, and so on. They paid much less attention to public participation and, above all, to the growth of human social and political capacity through participation. Much less was their emphasis on how people with social disadvantages relating to class, caste, gender, or race had grown, through participation in various economic and political processes, to build their social and political capacity, and thereby compensate for what they did not have by virtue of birth or background.

In development economics, Paul Streeten (1982, 1994, 1998), Mahbub ul Haq (1995), and Amartya Sen (1994) sought to reintroduce the importance of human development. They put *human beings* back into the development equation and maintained that there is much more to development than national income and its distribution. They broadened and deepened the notion of social and economic development. Amartya Sen, in particular, included in his notion of development the need for democracy as insurance against the callous policies of people in power.

The historical and cultural development of each society imposes its own social disadvantage on different sections of people. This, in turn, does injustice to those people and also devastates their human capacity to fight back. In such cases, it is not enough to say that their human development will be secured by education, health, and training in skills. For such segments of society you have also to devise ways of building their sense of self-worth as human beings. In some of the hierarchically ordered societies like India, those who were regarded as untouchables, for instance, were made to feel inferior through an adroit use of karmic rationale by the upper castes. Since the untouchables were a source of cheap agricultural labor, the upper castes always made the point that it was the *karma* of past life that made them what they were in this life. The untouchables, in their view, should question the makers of us all rather than blame the upper castes. More than three thousand years of recorded history of Indian civilization had made the untouchables deeply internalize those arguments. And when they were given opportunities through various affirmative programs and policies, they could not make full use of them. They need social activists to guide them to the provisions of such policies.

Furthermore, the social activists, and the woefully slow leadership of the downtrodden, were not enough to build back their sense of self-worth. They needed a process of social and economic self-involvement, within the broader community of which they were a part, to rejuvenate themselves as human beings. Electoral processes for constituting public authority at the village, sub-district, and district level, where they could get involved and exercise their vote, provided such a participatory opportunity. It was, nevertheless, difficult for them to connect their human development through such processes. What helped them much more, not only in the growth of their political capacity but also in their full ethnodevelopment in general, was the participatory opportunity connected with their livelihood. The milk cooperative movement in India established institutions at the grassroots level that connected participation with livelihood. By means of their involvement in those institutions, these socially disadvantaged segments of Indian society—which included the former untouchables, the tribals, and women—got an opportunity for self-development and thereby gradually altered their traditional social and economic relationships that had condemned them to an inferior and subhuman status. Some of those opportunities, at least initially, were not intended to benefit them. It was merely a fortuitous combination of circumstances that brought socially concerned cooperative dairy personnel and social activists to help the disadvantaged benefit from such opportunities at the grassroots level.

The concept of human development thus needs to be examined not only from the perspective of policy and provision of services, but also from the point of view of involvement in participatory processes for those who are at a social and economic disadvantage. If disadvantaged groups are mere recipients of what is legislated, their political capacity is not increased. Such capacity is a prerequisite to their becoming demanders and takers of what may be rightfully theirs. In its absence they will continue to depend on bureaucrats for the installment of benefits. Rather, if they are involved in a participatory process, their self-esteem and political capacity will grow and, as a result, they will move toward equal citizenship.

Such a process of growing up to one's full selfhood, and assurance of equality of opportunity in a community of participating individuals, also ensures that one would look to development opportunities in the same way as do others in one's community. Something like adult franchise which provides everyone with equal voting opportunity. In this case, equal development opportunities to take one's rightful place in a community where everyone is expected to benefit by means of an equality of opportunity. For this, no doubt some prior groundwork—by way of education, affirmative action policies, and socially concerned individuals initially guiding them—will be necessary. But once past those stages, there is a possibility of such individuals blossoming out into their own, like any other member of society. Of course, there will be some among them who would continue to be perpetual wards, but limited duration of affirmative policy benefits should be able to keep them in check.

In this chapter, we shall delve deeper into the concept of human development by exploring whether the involvement of underprivileged people in the milk cooperative movement enabled them to chip away at traditional social disadvantages. We should add here that participation in the institutions set up by the movement was substantially different from participation in the village panchayat (council). In the latter, people could squabble among themselves and be indifferent to the outcome because the panchayat was concerned only in a limited way with the administration of the local community. That was not the case, however, with the village milk cooperative because it was connected to people's livelihood. The presence of such a dimension made the participatory process in milk cooperatives far more important to all members. At times, the participatory process of cooperatives also made a difference to the panchayat because the same people were involved in running the two institutions.

The democratic experiences of grassroots institutions such as milk cooperatives need to be considered with reference to the variety of goals pursued. For the sake of convenience, we can divide such goals into three categories: primary goals, which aimed at enrolling new members and increasing milk production. Secondary goals, which attended to, directly or indirectly, the economic development of the disadvantaged, including women. And tertiary goals, which referred to going beyond milk to issues such as health, education, agricultural cooperatives, etc. In this chapter, we will consider importance of these goals to both Amul and the NDDB, their growing perception of the interrelationships of these goals, and the rationale that these two organizations offered in prioritizing these goals.

Since Amul and then the NDDB had spearheaded the milk cooperative movement in India, the grassroots institutions established by them and the democratic experience they had gained, became the dominant influence on grassroots institutions elsewhere. There were also local adaptations, deviations, and differences. For a variety of reasons, they did not always function in their democratic governance the way the NDDB would have liked them to. And in some cases, as we shall see in this chapter, certain grassroots communities went beyond the expectations of the NDDB. In other communities the performance of such bodies was woefully short of what was expected as the minimum.

Initially, most of the goals were formulated and then implemented in a top-down flow sequence. But on occasions there was also a reversal of such a process when people at the base, with the help of social activists, goaded the decision-makers at the top to include in their policies what they thought was essential to their livelihood and well-being.

Since milk cooperatives were, by definition, about milk, enrolling new members and assisting them toward increasing milk production became the primary goal of the grassroots institutions. Apart from providing support for such goals by means of infrastructure of services and inputs, there was also an explicit statement regarding the kind of grassroots institutions that would serve those goals most effectively. This explicit statement embraced a political philosophy which maintained that wherever farmer-owned and operated institutions were established, with adequate participatory and accountability features in place, the cooperative institutions at all levels functioned most effectively and in the interest of the people who constituted them. Such a political philosophy was borne out of Amul's experience, which then became an article of faith with the NDDB when it was engaged in establishing such institutions in other parts of India.

Such rationale was also present in the secondary goal, which required milk cooperatives to become a factor in the economic development of the socially disadvantaged groups in rural society, including women. Finally, the tertiary goal, on which there was very little agreement or commitment, referred to going beyond milk to related areas or concerns. This tertiary goal remained at the level of vision translating itself into hope, and possibly, some day, into target. It was pursued only by the socially committed individuals of various unions or by social activists within the region who found grassroots milk cooperatives highly effective rural institutions to take the cooperative enterprise beyond milk into the related areas of grassroots concerns.

Tertiary goals, in a sense, were a logical deduction of the primary and secondary goals, but not everyone wanted to get involved in pursuing them. The goal of human healthcare, for instance, was the logical progression from animal healthcare. And barring Amul, other milk unions either hesitated to pursue it or were discouraged from doing so. Similarly, the drive for literacy among milk pouring women could be seen as helping the primary goal but was pursued only by the isolated rural communities of Rajasthan. Valsad pursued the problem of sanitation and hygiene, also closely connected with human health and quality of milk. Then there was the consumers' cooperative, whereby the principle of eliminating the middlemen from milk extended to attempting to do the same with articles of daily use. Father Berechi in Bharuch-Surat district attempted to do this. Then there was the utilization of the milk cooperatives' resources to help out farmers in distress as a result of drought: a goal pursued by Banas, Sabar, and Mehsana. Valsad also had the most ambitious program of involving more and more women in dairying not just as a showpiece, but as actual managers. It proposed the women's micro savings and lending groups, which, to a large extent, were confined to men in Mehsana. But Sumul envisaged the most ambitious program concerning tertiary goals. There, top management thought that the new economic community, created by milk cooperatives at the grassroots level, could be put to use to solve a wider range of problems that plagued the people in rural areas.

Since the focus of this chapter is on participatory institutions, which the milk cooperatives put in place in order to pursue their goals, we shall concentrate on the democratic and human self-building components of the institutions. The expression "human self-building" here refers to the diminished sense of self-worth on the part of the lower economic and social strata of rural society, which includes women. Over the years, through social indignities, exclusions, and an adroit use of *karmic* rational, they were made to feel that they did not matter much to their society.

Later in this chapter we will examine the pressures on those institutions to go beyond their primary concerns of milk. We shall discuss these and other issues under the following subheadings: (I) The "Anand Pattern" of Democracy; (II) Cooperatives Define Democracy; (III) Large Farmers' Democracy; (IV) Small Farmers' Empowerment Process; (V) Political Empowerment Preceded the Economic; (VI) The Democratic Intermediaries; (VII) Policy Implementing Democracy; (VIII) Cooperatives and Liberalization; and finally, (IX) An Emerging Cooperative Democracy.

I. The "Anand Pattern" of Democracy

Milk cooperatives of India, at their very inception, built participatory institutions at the grassroots level. During the final phase of struggle against the colonial administration, from 1942 to 1946, the demand for milk cooperatives was seen as one that would institutionalize one's right to sell one's agricultural products to a body that would protect one's interests rather than government-appointed contractors. What began as a demand for rights in milk business reflected a wider claim for the variety of rights embodied in the struggle for national independence. Such a normative demand for rights was later seen as a good policy. Policy makers can and should be held accountable provided the right to elect them in the first place exists. That way, if voters are active and vigilant, their interests may be enhanced and protected.

From the colonial days, Indian milk producers' experience of working under a government bureaucracy and its chief executive, the milk commissioner, was not a happy one. In fact, the bureaucracy was not only obstructive and unaccountable, but also was hostile to grassroots initiatives. Added to this, in the postcolonial period, was corruption. There are still a large number of milk cooperative institutions in India, which are run on such lines. They serve the interests of bureaucracy and the political class, first, and then those of their cooperative constituents. So the logical response to counter such a deficiency was to establish grassroots milk cooperatives that were run on participatory lines and to which elected and appointed officials would be held accountable. Later on, such cooperatives came to be known as "Anand Pattern" milk cooperatives.

In that connection, it must be said to the credit of both Amul and, subsequently, the NDDB that they correctly diagnosed, a long time ago, that India had a milk problem. Neither the private enterprise nor the state-run bureaucracy was able to give a fair deal to producers and a quality product to consumers. In fact, both of them had failed miserably in the milk industry.

According to folklore, the Indian milk industry has been known as the most corrupt form of business, given that milk can be easily diluted with water. In order to overcome this, Amul and the NDDB did not take the usual Indian route of handing the problem over to the state bureaucracy. They decided to put milk producers in charge of running cooperative institutions that would not only procure milk from far and near villages within the district, but also appoint professional managers to process it, market it, and give the producers the best return possible.

In this respect they shared Gandhi's distrust of handing over responsibility to the state where individuals, cooperatively, could do better. Gandhi, actively involved in Indian freedom movement, did not have time to think through this third alternative of cooperative initiatives. But he had envisioned that if people were brought together across India's social, economic, and religious divides, they would solve many of their own problems. The very act of coming together for a common purpose would generate many acts of coop-eration. It was this vision he had passed on to his followers such as Sardar Patel, Morarji Desai, and a countless number of district level leaders. Moreover, in Gandhi's time, in colonial India in particular, there was no possibility of bringing the state into economic enter-prise. Britain rigidly controlled all operations of the state. Nehru, the socialist, after the end of colonial administration, was the first to use that option. And he used it extensively. But Gandhi, Gandhians, and neo-Gandhians like JP and his followers, were deeply apprehen-sive of such an alternative. JP thought through this and even wrote a book on the subject entitled *A Plea for the Reconstruction of Indian Polity* (Narayan n.d.).

In a sense, Amul, and later the NDDB, were cast in the Neo-Gandhian mold without agreeing with its other ideological inclinations. For the founding fathers of Amul, right from day one, the private milk traders were as much of a problem as the milk commissioners appointed by the colonial administration. And the alternative to these two was to have farmer-owned and farmer-oper-ated milk cooperatives. But these were easier to design theoretically than to put into practice. The majority of milk producers at the grassroots level did not know what such cooperatives were all about. Then there were the politicians and bureaucrats, who were keen on controlling, directly or indirectly, any public institution that might be useful to them politically or financially. And their hands were strengthened because the district bodies of milk cooperatives had to have nominees of the state in the name of protecting the public interest. The irony here was that elected members of state legislatures, some of whom were ministers, wanted to interfere with the working of grassroots bodies, which were also elected. They exercised the privilege of appointing "government nominees" to district level bodies. Given the archaic nature of legislative acts that governed cooperative structures in India, democratically elected, state-level representatives did not respect the democratically elected representatives at the district or union level. It became a case of one democracy raiding the other. The ministers in charge of cooperatives often appointed IAS (Indian Administrative Service) officials who were likely to do their bidding as managing directors or chairmen of the district level bodies. Some state ministers also got their sons elected to the chairmanship of unions. The result was that neither these bureaucrats nor politicians were accountable to cooperative members for whom they were supposed to work.[5]

In the tussle between the elected representatives of the grassroots communities and the politically and bureaucratically appointed top officials, the former were at a disadvantage. The grassroots communities in such cases had to wage a struggle not only against the bureaucrats, but also against politicians who were elected to the legislature by the people themselves. Only those states that had a tradition of having participated in the struggle for Indian independence, or had produced a leadership that strongly supported the cooperative movement, and/or were joined by social activists whenever the problem of interference arose, were successful in opposing the combination of corrupt politicians and bureaucrats. Elsewhere, the politicians and bureaucrats did inestimable harm to grassroots institutions.

This point was illustrated in Chapter 1 with reference to Tamil Nadu. To summarize here, elected politicians, through their appointees in the top positions, started interfering with the price mechanisms of milk in order to win elections in urban areas. In Tamil Nadu the price of milk was often half of what it was in other parts of India. The major cooperative milk unions often determined the price of milk on their own, keeping in mind what they thought was fair and what the market would be able to bear. As a result, they were able to give better prices to producers, nearly 75 percent of whom were small or marginal farmers or landless workers. Furthermore, because of this better price, milk producers stayed in the dairy industry and also attracted others who either had limited resources or were resourceless. But the politicians and bureaucrats did not even care to know who they had harmed or by how much. Their interference often resulted in court action, but the courts did not always support the cause of elected milk cooperatives.

One of the basic questions in this connection is how very genuinely *participatory* are the various grassroots milk cooperative institutions? Even if there were regular elections in primary milk cooperatives, and their office bearers elected representatives to higher bodies, and then those, in turn, elected members of the board; can it be taken for granted that genuine participation was at work when those people were elected? No doubt, the process of *participation* is put to work when various organizations elect their representatives, but then there are other questions. Economically developed and politically conscious states such as Gujarat, where milk cooperatives first struck roots, launched a genuine grassroots movement and saw to it that its villages had elected milk coopera- tive institutions. But most of the other states, where milk cooperative dairying had spread, depended upon the technocrats of the NDDB to impress upon state governments of the need to hold elections and constitute various bodies on participatory lines. In fact, they were required to sign an undertaking that they would abide by the requirements of Anand Pattern milk cooperative insti- tutions.

The formal commitment of the NDDB to democratic principles and participation was taken a step further when it established a

Department of Cooperative Development. One of the major responsibilities of this department was to build a team consisting of NDDB's experienced staff, and people recruited locally and trained by the NDDB, to inculcate the values of democratic participation by means of seminars and workshops. Later on, that body also took over the responsibility of initiating more women into the decision making bodies at the grassroots level. The program of involving more women subsequently sought to empower women in various ways.

There were periodic evaluations of the program by NDDB staff as well as outside scholars. As an organization, and also as a body of trained instructors, the NDDB and local workers did an admirable job of making people aware of the need to participate in decision making in local cooperatives.

What they could not do, and did not want to do, however, was to let milk producers, who were increasingly drawn from the lower economic and social strata of rural society, engage in their own self-directed, participatory exercises. The well-meaning staff of the NDDB often tried to save them from attempting trial-and-error exercises. History tells us that participatory citizenship comes about through self-involvement and that trial-and-error exercises lead to a greater understanding of what participation is all about. An overprotective approach to participants often limits their ability to learn useful lessons about participation by going wrong sometimes, and then engaging in course corrections by themselves. In other words, involvement in the participatory process builds a more experienced and politically evolved citizenry than participation undertaken at the behest of more educated, knowledgeable, and socially concerned technologists.

Here it could be argued that rural India did not have the time to lose more than it already had. The NDDB had been training grassroots milk producers for nearly a quarter of a century in cooperative self-governance. And that had produced some good results. It should therefore be allowed to continue its time-tested approach.

However, in such an approach—whereby NDDB technologists guide grassroots communities—one thing was missing: learning to defend participatory institutions whenever bureaucrats and/or politicians either ignored them or transgressed against their established procedures and rights.

Furthermore, since the milk producers themselves did not always engage in a struggle to win participatory institutional provisions in the first place, they were much less prepared to be able to defend them. Consequently, during the period of infraction of democratic process, the milk producers were unable to resist on their own. They had to look to NDDB's guidance, court action, and various lobbying efforts to overcome such problems. When chief ministers, agriculture ministers, or senior bureaucrats committed infractions against either the participatory provisions or the unstated norms underlying them, the grassroots communities had no other recourse but to turn to the people who had established those participatory institutions in the first place. At such moments, they looked to the NDDB to add its voice to their struggle against politicians and bureaucrats. In this connection, one could certainly argue with justification that it was too early in India's evolving democracy to expect such people to defend their participatory rights by themselves. At the same time, however, it cannot be denied that one learns about the value of participatory institutions when one is directly involved in defending them.

II.   Cooperatives Define Democracy

The NDDB had initially tried to define what kind of cooperative body it wanted to set up at the grassroots, union, and state level and then, after a few years, operationally grapple with the problem of democratic governance within those institutions. One of the persons who was at the center of the first round of deliberations, was Dr. S.N. Singh who, until recently, occupied the position of director of the program for Cooperative Development at the NDDB. The question that the team under him, and Dr. N. Belavadi, examined in 1987 was why were the cooperatives not receiving from state governments the kind of response they had expected? One of the explanations they came up with was narrated to us in a personal communication with Dr. Singh, February 6, 2000: "The realization dawned that probably we have gone too fast in organizing the dairy (and other) cooperatives with reasonable levels of success." At that stage, they were inclined to blame themselves rather than the bizarre democratic mutant that rural India had become whereby, in a manner of speaking, the children of higher democracy were eating up the children of lower democracy. The duly elected representatives of the people at the state level were either obstructing the creation of corresponding democratic structures at the grassroots and/or district level or filling the positions within them with their families and friends to get direct and indirect benefits. The politicians at the state level were out to resist the spread of democratic institutions lower down if they could not control them or get benefits out of them. That was an unacceptable behavior. It also flew in the face of a commonsensical view that individuals who occupied public office by virtue of electoral support stayed out of each other's ways. That is to say that with democracy also came a normative commitment of respecting each other's representative position. But here was an exception that did not want a democracy if it could not be manipulated. As long as the existing legislation governing cooperatives was not amended, the political class, with servile bureaucrats supporting it, could always subvert the will of the same people who put them in the position of power in the first place. It was neither the "speed" nor the "spread" of cooperatives that had caused the obstruction. It was just the strange behavior of a class of politicians who wanted to monopolize power and the potential political benefits associated with the cooperatives.

The major problem seemed to be that the politicians were unwilling to give an autonomous status to cooperatives. Under the guise of "public interest" they wanted to control the cooperatives.

And as the milk cooperatives generated more revenue and gave employment to more people, the elected politicians could not resist the temptation of appointing or having their own men elected either as chairmen, managing directors, or contractors for supplying materials and transport facilities.

Then there were other problems such as the lack of cooperative development. This was reflected in the lack of cooperative member loyalty, a low level of participation, the absence of professional management, a lack of accountability, the misuse of funds, and so on. The question was whether the NDDB staff could develop a Cooperative Mission, with definite strategies for educating and preparing members for greater participation, regular elections, and meetings. Further, the NDDB staff recognized they needed strategies to motivate the staff, develop a code of conduct, increase women's membership, and make members aware that cooperatives could not be run democratically, in the interest of their members, unless they possessed true autonomy. The NDDB thus had didactic aims, attempting to make its grassroots bodies more participatory and vigilant against the abuse of power and outside interference.

The next step for the NDDB was to recruit staff, train them, and ask them to go into the field and help the grassroots bodies build a democratic ethos. But how do you guarantee that the elected men of India would respect this democratic ethos? They had already been elected to positions of public trust and only the following election could displace them. Here, they could always count on the short memory of the people. So then you are back to where you had started, namely, build the average constituent of milk cooperatives to observe democratic ideals. Indeed, this was a tall order but worth trying, at least with sections of the rural community. This led to the NDDB's preference for educating the women among them, hoping that they, the women, would better absorb the ideals of democratic behavior and offer resistance when those ideals were violated (NDDB 1991:2-3).

The NDDB, being primarily an economic institution, had hesitated to take the ultimate step of reorienting its cooperative development programs around the ideals of participatory and democratic governance. There was always the fear that political parties and politicians in power would *politicize* the grassroots community for some electoral gains. Given the widespread abuse of elected positions, democracy in India has not so far been able to rehabilitate one of its central functions, namely, *public service.* All successful democracies have been able to attract deserving people who genuinely believe that they would like to give a few years of their lives to public service. They also believe that what they have to give can make a difference. Almost all of them have experienced the problem of finding a balance between their private interest and public interest, which has to be brought about in the domain of legality, propriety, and morality (Somjee 1986:29-31). In India at this stage, however, while there is a widespread condemnation of the "venality" of the political class, the thinking men and women have yet to address the central problem of their democracy: how should private and public interests be balanced and, further, how will transgressions on the part of the political class be monitored? In this sense, the grassroots communities experience, at their level, what the country at large is also facing.

III.   Large Farmers' Democracy

In *Designs For Democracy: Building Energetic Farmers' Organisations* (1992), Tushar Shah and his colleagues discuss how farmers have been able to establish cooperative institutions, succeed economically, and run them democratically to protect their own interests. Shah makes a distinction between cooperatives, on the one hand, and trade and industry associations on the other. For Shah, the basic attraction of cooperatives is "the services and outputs produced" by them. Cooperatives for him are "member-organizations," and therefore the members manage them. They also have self-governance, equality, and voluntarism. To the members of cooperatives, equality and voluntarism are as important as self-governance. Each of these plays an important part in the successful functioning of cooperatives. Most of the cooperatives that India has were, in fact, created by "government fiat" or by means of a "normative principle" implying that it is good to have cooperatives. Such a position undermines voluntarism. Cooperatives imposed from the top, therefore, have a slim chance of success.

With reference to cooperatives, Shah uses the Sanskrit concept of *swaymbhoo,* which means "self-creation." In building cooperatives, a group of individuals band themselves together on their own, make their own rules, and define how they are going to protect their interests. Cooperatives survive as long as members are convinced that they operate to serve their interests. Shah explains, "Utility to members is the only basis for co-operatives to emerge and sustain; and the only normative rules that might have use for co-operative are those which demonstrably enhance its ability to achieve purposes important to members better than alternative organizations" (Shah et al. 1992:6).

For Shah, social structure, regional culture, and political economy are of little importance to the success of cooperatives. Most important are what he calls "design concepts," presumably meaning institutions. One needs appropriate institutions for cooperatives, and this will go a long way in ensuring their operational success. These institutions can be conceived, operated, and developed only by those who voluntarily come together to protect their interests and act as equals.

Taking issue with Professors Baviskar and Attwood, who attribute the success of cooperatives to regional political economy and culture, especially in Maharashtra and Gujarat, Shah argues that he has seen successful cooperatives in the Periyar district in south India, which flourished for a decade and then disappeared. The same was true of some cooperatives in Tamil Nadu and Andhra Pradesh. So, according to Shah, the characterization of Gujarat and Maharashtra as fertile grounds for cooperatives in every respect is wrong.

Shah tested his design concept thesis in Surat district first, and found that there was something to be said about the local culture that helped a large number of flourishing cooperatives, which went back 85 years or more, and which covered a range of agricultural products. The presence of such a local culture may have provided certain operative norms to individuals who came together to pursue their common interests. But then you could not stretch the local culture argument too far, because Kheda district, a region with the same culture, did not have much success in fields other than dairying.

Shah singled out Surat and also Valsad districts for having produced some of the best cooperatives in India. For him, their secret of success was that wherever Patidars dominated the scene, they brought the characteristics of being calculating, practical, and given to orderly life. The Patidars made their money first and engaged in what he called "co-operative philanthropies," which implied that others, too, must have such an opportunity. But then the same was not true of Patidars everywhere, according to him (Shah et al. 1992:20-26). According to Shah, the "Sugar cooperatives in South Gujarat succeeded because they hit upon a design concept which struck admirable concordance between member goals, the co-operative's central purpose, the design of its operating system and of its political structures and processes" (Shah et al. 1992:64-65).

Moreover, sugar cane cooperatives of South Gujarat are "closed" cooperatives, where no more new members are accepted and even the elections are intensely fought. They also stay true to the vision of their founding members and rarely deviate from this. To them "design concept" is important because it serves the purposes for which cooperatives were put in place. It was because of their design concept that by 1991, Surat and Bulsar [Valsad] had 10 out of 14 successful cooperatives (Shah et al. 1992:124-134).

Shah's "design concept" may be useful in explaining the cooperatives of rich farmers. And up to a point Shah is also correct in stating that Kurien and T.K. Patel succeeded in milk because of their "design concept," which combined vision with operative efficiency and members' interests. But there was much more to their effort; they also successfully replicated milk cooperatives in half the number of districts in India where milk producers joined because cooperatives served their interest and also because there were socially concerned individuals coming from the milk unions and/or the NDDB that they could trust. Subsequently, in some villages and districts, they also encouraged grassroots leadership to work closely with union leaders, veterinarians, and, in some cases, with Christian missionaries; and all of them showed great concern for the welfare of members. Amazingly, however, Surat and Valsad, through such individuals, built milk cooperatives among the tribals who had no idea of what the "design concept" in the union headquarters was. In 2004, nearly 80 percent of the milk collected was from their tribal villages.

Unlike sugarcane, fruits and vegetables, cotton, and tobacco cooperatives, milk cooperatives were essentially the cooperatives of small and marginal farmers with an increasing membership coming from the landless. Prior to joining the milk cooperatives and, subsequently, in operating their grassroots institutions and expanding them, a lot of socially concerned individuals had provided help. One could therefore say with equal emphasis that while considerations of helping out the helpless had no place in rich men's cooperatives, the poor man's cooperatives very nearly rested on that foundation. And while individuals in rich men's cooperatives could look after their own interests; it was important to build the social and political capacity of those who had remained outside the mainstream of Indian economic and political life by involving them in democratic processes of the grassroots cooperatives. The milk cooperatives thus became schools for learning how democracy works, while also protecting the interests of members in the most practical manner. At that level, it was not merely a theoretical exercise, but one that was tied to livelihood.

IV. The Empowerment Process of Small Farmers

If we examine the various speeches of the former chairman of the NDDB, Dr. V. Kurien, we find that his initial emphasis was on establishing milk cooperatives for the milk producers. And if some-one did not have the means, or as they say in Gujarat villages, *sadhan,* then he or she was out of luck. Such an emphasis was natural in the early days of building milk cooperatives and making them produce results for their members. But as the NDDB gained experience in building such cooperatives, it also realized that within the social queue there were changes occurring at both ends of the milk producing community. Medium and large landowners, who were significantly involved in milk cooperatives in the beginning, were either reducing their investment in milch animals or getting out of it altogether. Simultaneously, at the other end of the social queue, small and marginal farmers, and even landless laborers, were joining. Consequently, without a formal shift in policy of the organizers, the local situation in grassroots communities and in various unions, compelled the organizers to pay more attention to inducting the small landowners, the landless, the tribals, and so on, into their respective milk producing communities. Moreover, various kinds of subsidies and grants also helped rural people acquire the *sadhan* to become milk producers.

This shift was quite gradual, and at times not without its own heart-warming drama of helping those who were initially "left out." Consider the following four examples.

First, the highly successful milk cooperative of Pamol, in Dudhsagar's jurisdiction in Mehsana (which had become a mega milk economy), had compassion towards the landless. It therefore built on its own village common the *gaucher* (a fodder farm) with help from Australian aid agencies. The fodder farm provided a steady livelihood to a number of landless laborers, and also a head load of farm cuttings, the *bharo*, to each of them over and above their wages. This enabled them to maintain milch animals by supplementing the fodder with cattle feed. They then entered the milk producing community of the village and started gaining an extra income. As more and more water became available by means of bore wells in this mega milk village, more and more landless laborers were employed. Each of these was entitled to bring a *bharo* home and maintain an animal.

Second, the economic and human revolution brought about by both Surat and Valsad, by building milk cooperatives in adivasi villages where they neither had milch animals nor a culture of drinking milk, was quite stunning. In the year 2004, these highly successful milk unions had close to 80 percent of their milk collection coming from tribal villages, which, twenty-five years ago, hardly sent any to the union.

Third, the milk union of Kolhapur, in Maharashtra, faced great resistance from the upper castes in letting its Dalits become members of common or "all-caste" milk cooperatives. And instead of throwing up their hands in defeat, the organizers of the milk union opted for the successful alternative of allowing the Dalits to have their own 400 flourishing milk cooperatives, which gave them a steady income.

Fourth, the example of Sabar is full of irony. It had to persuade the Patidars of a prosperous subdistrict called Prantij to establish milk cooperatives so that the lower social and economic groups could emulate them and enter dairying. Initially, the Patidars were not keen on this idea, but they went along with the request. In the year 2000, it was the non-Patidar producers that met the bulk of Sabar's milk requirements.

We could provide additional examples from Bihar, Rajasthan, Tamil Nadu, Karnataka, and elsewhere, where the nature of the milk producing community had started to change, but not without the socially concerned efforts of either the villagers themselves, the staff of milk unions, and/or social activists.

The point to be made is that the milk cooperative movement in India established institutions at the grassroots level and also at the district level, which had to be operated democratically. Those communities did not have the fierce individualism, education, business acumen, and ability to implement the democratic process to protect their interests, as did the rich men's cooperatives in Surat and Valsad, which Shah described. The question was how does one overcome such a disadvantage? The answer is found in the context-effective measures that were available and adopted. Socially concerned individuals, either in the form of social activists from the region or the deeply committed staff of the various unions, or grass-roots leadership itself, made a difference by giving their time and effort to building milk cooperatives and making them work. And, in the process, they had prepared the cooperative members, increasingly, to play their own important part.

V. Political Empowerment Preceded Economic Empowerment

Since before Indian independence, political forces have either preceded or gone hand in hand with economic forces. This was also true of the Indian national movement, which had started in the mid-nineteenth century and which had put as much emphasis on political change as on economic employment. Often, political change, which could be far more focused during the struggle for independence, outpaced economic employment. That particular sequence had continued during the half century following Indian independence. In their many-faceted development, the Indians have never ceased to be a "politics first" people. The emphasis on economic development first and then on democracy, which was followed in countries such as South Korea, Taiwan, Japan, and Indonesia, was significantly absent in India. When the former president of Indonesia, Suharto, uttered the famous slogan "Development before Politics," Indians were suspicious of his motives.

The well-known development scholars, S.P. Huntington and Joan Nelson, in their book *No Easy Choice* (1976), explained that there are irreversible sequences that follow each choice, development and politics. Scholars have yet to assess which choice in the short and long run seems best. Which of these two choices created more suffering for the people: the slow pace of economic growth, or the political instability resulting from the lack of political participation?

The Indians, true to their "politics first" passion, empowered their entire citizenry with universal adult franchise as soon as they became independent, much in advance of the demand for it. In that sense, they had shared the vision and idealism of the liberal political philosophers of the West, from John Locke to John Dewey. Their thinking and faith implied that once given an opportunity to participate, the individual, no matter how socially and economically deprived, would quickly learn how to protect and advance his or her interests.

It is true that many Indians maintained this faith in liberal individualism. Indira Gandhi made an attempt to undo democracy, but Indians disgraced her at the polls and taught her a lesson. As the lower strata of the hierarchically ordered Indian society entered the democratic arena, they trusted their ethnic leaders to voice their demands for economic opportunities. Regrettably, those ethnic leaders resorted to corruption and nepotism. There was precious little that the lower strata could do. Most of them waited patiently for such ethnic leaders to change or for someone else from their rank to question and replace them.

One affluent group, however, felt that enough was enough and started toying with the idea of ending the soft democracy of India. Since it came from Bombay it was dubbed the "Bombay Club." This group became impatient with India's *desi* (indigenous) style of democracy, which, according to it had become a "farce" under the thrust of the *Mandalization* (reserving jobs and due importance in politics for people of socially and economically backward groups) of Indian politics. The preference of the Bombay Club, which wanted to compete with the best in the world in this age of globalization, was for a "soft autocracy" (Dilip and Bobb 1994). Not many believed in the efficacy of a soft autocracy. Over time, individuals within the Bombay club settled for whatever political deals they could get from various political parties.

The milk cooperatives of India, however, did not lose their faith in democracy. The NDDB's emphasis on Anand Pattern milk cooperatives reflected the faith of the founding fathers of the Indian republic in the ability of individuals to rise above their limitations and, through public participation, learn to effectively guard their own interests. In this sense, the Anand Pattern cooperatives, with all their emphasis on election of office-bearers, attempted to introduce an economic democracy that was bound to be taken far more seriously than the political democracy of the panchayat because people's livelihood depended on them (Somjee and Somjee 1978). Just as the broader democratic process in India was expected to become an enabling process for those involved; the involvement of the milk producer in the grassroots participatory process of milk cooperatives, no matter how limited, was to become an enabling or empowering process. It is true that such a process gave no guarantee that the political capacity of the individual would grow, but involvement in the grassroots democratic process was indeed a step-by-step incremental process. It was tortuously slow and sometimes messy. In helping to operate grassroots cooperative institutions, the socially concerned staff of the NDDB, the unions, and social activists showed great patience and perseverance. In different parts of India, their influence was unmistakable. To their democratic coaching we now turn.

VI.   The Democratic Intermediaries

If we look closely at the growth of the political capacity of the various social segments in India, we find that the earliest among them to develop, during the colonial rule, were the nationalist leaders and those in the legal profession who defended them. These leaders initially operated through prayers and petitions, asking the colonial rulers for representation in legislative bodies, on the one hand, and employment opportunities on the other. In different parts of India there were groups that were impatient, wanting to hasten the end of colonial rule and they, sometimes, engaged in violence. Usually, however, Indians operated within the rule of law while putting forward their demands. It was a trying time for both sides. Finally, the defining moment came when Gandhi turned the movement into a mass *satygrahic* (non-violent) movement, asserting that Britain must quit India. It began in 1920. The movement launched by Gandhi enabled a large number of people overcome their fear of opposing the government of the day. The movement thus helped them to not only get involved in a political process, but also to grow in their political capacity. Nearly three decades of the non-violent movement in different parts of India snowballed into a vast army of new, politically empowered people whose main achievement was overcoming the fear of their armed rulers. The political equation between the people and the rulers was irrevocably altered. The mass movement, launched by Gandhi, increased the political capacity of large number of people and prepared them to share the responsibility of running democratic institutions on both sides of the power divide.

Despite being a mass movement, it could not influence every person in the country. People had to find other ways to gain access to the political process. This occurred when democratic institutions were created at five different levels: village, subdistrict, district, state, and center. This gave many Indians the opportunity to learn how to be a part of the Indian democratic process and, thereby, grow in their political capacity.

In rural areas in particular, the first people to take part were mainly those with large landholdings. But each subsequent election brought people from the lower strata into the electoral fray. Involvement in this process has yet to give the lowest strata of rural society their fullest sense of inclusion and empowerment, so they can use their votes to achieve their major social and economic objectives. In urban areas, the educated and the professionals made use of meetings, lobbies, media, and the courts to learn how to exercise their democratic freedoms and rights. Such an *ethnopolitical* development in a democracy is a continuous process. Elected rulers and decision-making bodies do not want to be solely responsible or accountable to those who elect them. After being elected, they want to enjoy the fruits of office, status, and power, and the demanding citizenry is always regarded as a thorn in their side.

In the democratic institutions created by Anand Pattern cooperatives, the small and marginal farmers, the landless, the tribals, and all the socially disadvantaged groups including women, needed encouragement to get involved in the participatory processes of those institutions. In different parts of India encouragement had come through different kinds of, what may be termed "democratic intermediaries." The growth of milk cooperatives, and the involvement in democratic process within them, was unthinkable without the help and perseverance of such intermediaries.

Over the years T.K. Patel and Motibhai Chaudhury assiduously set up democratic institutions in their respective districts of Kheda and Mehsana. Patel even asked the Patidars to take along *the nabado varg* (weaker section) in their decision-making. Motibhai Chaudhury, and Mansinhbhai earlier, with their ceaseless efforts, encouraged the Chaudhuries of Mehsana villages, often considered to be a backward people, to pay attention to the changing techniques of dairying and participate fully in the democratic process of their grassroots communities. They were thus not only building inclusive institutions, but also encouraging people to participate in them.

In addition, the veterinarians of Mehsana targeted the weaker sections of villages to not only involve them in dairying, but also in the decision-making processes of their institutions. Dr. A.S. Dave, a senior veterinarian, spent more time in the villages than at his desk at the union office, where he was equally needed. Similar work was done by Dr. H.A. Ghasia, a veterinarian in Surat, and by Suresh Desai and Bina Desai, the two administrators in Valsad. Furthermore, socially concerned employees of the NDDB also performed similar services wherever they were sent. Dr. Vengankar and Dr. Ghanekar helped the Kolhapur union in the difficult transition from a government run cooperative to an Anand Pattern cooperative. Dr. Nadiadwala and Dr. Roychaudhury kept the democratic process going in the Bihar cooperatives under trying conditions. And while on the topic of trying conditions, it should be noted that Dr. Daniel and Dr. Nunes kept the democratic process going in the milk cooperatives of Tamil Nadu despite interference from the state government. Dr. N. Belavadi helped the leaders of grassroots communities in Karnataka make their democratic process more effective. These are the particular individuals whose activities we have watched in the field for a long time. But there were countless others who did equally distinguished work that we were not privileged to know, as we could not visit their areas of assignment. Father Ipye, Father Berechi, and Father Francis, in their own way, kept the tribals of Surat district involved in its grassroots democratic process.

Finally, with regard to the milk cooperatives of South Gujarat and their excellent work among tribals and women, we must not forget to mention the work done by Gandhians, JPians, and the new generation of NGOs. They literally ensured the democratic process and facilitated the increasing involvement of the poorer strata. In both Surat and Valsad districts, they worked tirelessly to encourage the weaker section to become, and remain, a part of the democratic process of the grassroots communities.

Earlier, these districts had benefited by the quiet work done by what we have called "Valod-Vedachi-Volunteerism." Valod and Vedachi are the two small towns in Surat district and a large number of social activists have come from there. South Gujarat was the theatre of peaceful non-violent resistance during the colonial days. After South Africa, Gandhi tried out a number of non-violent resistance movements in this region. And here, intense social activism is still a living tradition. Prosperous landowners, lawyers, industrialists, businessmen, schoolteachers, before and after their retirement, involve themselves in cottage industries and income generating schemes for the poor. The famous *Lijjat Papad* has received help and support from the local social activists. These activists have also encouraged members of milk cooperatives to participate in their democratic process.

These socially active individuals brought the weaker sections of rural communities into dairying and encouraged them to stay in it and take more interest in its workings. These people, who come from a variety of backgrounds, acted as democratic intermediaries until the grassroots institutions were able to provide their own leaders. Once they were assured of such leadership, they moved on to other communities that needed their help. It is because of them that milk cooperatives came to be run democratically despite being institutions of the weaker sections of rural communities.

As elsewhere in the country, leaders played an important role in grassroots democracy. Nevertheless, they had to take into account the views of others, and remain accountable to them. In an adivasi village in Valsad, women threw out a chairperson who claimed too much credit for herself. They first defeated her in an election, then asked her elected rival to resign, and then re-elected the credit-claiming individual after she had moderated her claims. The chastened former chairperson was re-elected, as most members told us, because she was competent. What was happening in those grassroots democracies was of constant surprise to us as we got to know more about them.

The range of socially concerned individuals who got involved in establishing, operating, consolidating, and expanding milk cooperatives at the rural level, also helped, directly and indirectly, in making its implicit democratic process more acceptable to the people. It took some time for them to realize that their own interests could be defended and advanced provided they were involved in the participatory processes of those institutions.

These democratic intermediaries were guardians of the uninitiated, the poor, the socially marginalized, those lacking education, and so on. The intermediaries enabled these disadvantaged groups to go beyond the slots assigned to them by India's social hierarchy. They could not directly attack that society, but gradually nibble away at its fringes to emerge from the various social and economic disadvantages to which they were condemned for a long time. Universal adult suffrage certainly helped in the political field, but more was needed to be able to make a difference in the economic field. And this opportunity came to the countless villages of India wherever those socially concerned individuals were present and willing to play the role of democratic intermediaries, encouraging and guiding the disadvantaged towards new roles in grassroots democratic organizations.

VII. Policy—Implementing Democracy

There was yet another unexpected bonanza. With socially concerned milk technocrats, milk union staff, and a host of social activists operating in various districts, there was a good possibility of their supervising the implementation of policies that were put in place. That alone, at this stage of India's democratic development, could be seen as a major contribution. At the macro level, India, the world's largest democracy, is beginning to reveal a major drawback—it has become a "non-implementing" democracy. Elected representatives of state assemblies and the *Loksabha* formulate policy and embody them in legislation. And when it comes to their implementation they turn around and help rich and powerful individuals to dodge the law in return for cash and/or other favors. Here the elected politicians are not the only culprits. Administrators often join them in dodging the law. India therefore has now earned the notoriety of having become one of the most corrupt countries in the world.

At the grassroots level, given the presence of the democratic intermediaries and the increasingly empowered cooperative membership, such transgressions in areas covered by milk cooperatives are decreasing. In our fieldwork in different parts of rural India, we came across only a few instances of this kind of corruption. One such instance was in the Erode district in Tamil Nadu. The secretary of the milk cooperative, who was required to test the fat content of the milk poured, had a few unmarked bottles for milk with a lower fat content. He would then switch the bottles of the pourers for those with lower fat content, and then distribute the difference among three or four individuals who were involved in the scam. A highly educated, entrepreneurial pourer, who himself used to test his milk for its fat content, finally caught up with him. The secretary then pleaded that the political party in power had wanted him to commit these acts. Tamil Nadu, as stated earlier, had the notoriety of interfering with the business of milk cooperatives, which was unheard of in other parts of India.

Under the NDDB's instruction, and also under the milk unions' directives, there is now much-needed firmness in implementing policies. This firmness has created in the milk cooperatives a kind of rule of law, which is missing even in other cooperatives. By becoming law- and policy-implementing organizations, the grass-roots bodies connected with milk cooperatives have become very popular in villages of India.

In the grassroots milk cooperatives, then, this huge mass of Indian citizenry has learned that strict policy implementation, with-out exception, is in everybody's interest. It has also realized that it is the only way to strengthen India's democracy.

VIII. Cooperatives and Liberalization

Neither India nor the vast network of milk cooperatives within India lives in isolation from the rest of the world. Consequently, from 1991 onwards, India decided to move away from its economic policy of state control, which had not only held back its growth rate but also had prevented its rural poor from escaping poverty. Even during the state control of the economy, for more than forty years since independence, India had remained, at best, a mixed economy. Hence, the decision to dismantle the rigid state control restored other forms of economic activity including private enterprise and the cooperative sector. Fortunately, for the cooperative sector, the shift came at a time when it had started to prosper. The cooperative sector in milk, in particular, has already made India the top milk producing country in the world.

With the added economic opportunity also came the added pressure for competition in the cooperative sector. With the exception of milk, edible oil seeds, and cotton, most cooperatives were either the creations of government policies or were mired in politics, as was the case of the sugar cooperatives in Maharashtra. Even where the state control was more relaxed, elected politicians, to a small or large extent, either retained or extended their control over cooperatives in the name of the public interest.

For the grassroots milk cooperatives, the move to competition in the cooperative sector came a little too early. In the name of liberalization, elected politicians in Gujarat, Maharashtra, Karnataka, Tamil Nadu, Andhra Pradesh, and so on, hurriedly gave permission to private individuals to start milk companies. They were often started next door to the cooperatives without stringent regulations for veterinary and cattle feed services, which they were supposed to provide to milk producers. Then the central government did yet another disservice to the grassroots milk cooperatives by allowing milk multinationals to import highly subsidized milk powder, at a reduced tariff rate from developed countries. Nothing shook the faith of grassroots communities in their own elected officials more than this favor given to multinationals. Had the members of grassroots milk cooperatives been aggressive enough and threatened dire electoral consequences for the elected men, some politicians would have listened. The cooperative members did the next best thing and that is appeal to the courts. The courts in India, which have lost the confidence of the general public, believed that their role was to act only as interpreters of the law, rather than act as agents of social change. The NDDB was caught between the weakness of grassroots peasantry, not yet ready to assert its democratic rights, and an

160

unchanging judiciary, which increasingly looked like an extension of India's highly controversial bureaucracy.

In the winter of the year 2000, the NDDB went to the lawmakers asking them to let it function as a "producers' company," which would act autonomously and ask for no state support in return. This particular alternative has yet to play itself out in the contemporary development process of India. With this "sink or swim" alternative, milk cooperatives are likely to work harder to stay afloat. Some might, for a short time, go under. But their new role as a company might also stimulate democratic consolidation and convince elected politicians that policies should be formulated only after due consultations with the cooperatives. Their appeal to the elected politicians had been couched in the moral sense of "you ought to support cooperatives in the interests of the small farmers of India." That did not go very far. Nor can it be entirely ruled out that this widespread network of milk cooperatives may yet emerge as a farmers' political organization that will have a respectable number of seats in the state and central legislature. After that no body will ignore its interests. But there are also dangers. The new generation of cooperative politicians, sitting in legislative bodies, might ignore the interests of those they represent and play their own politics. Time alone will tell.

IX. An Emerging Cooperative Democracy

Ever since its inception, the NDDB has come in conflict with bureaucracy and elected politicians who want more power and/or favor, either for themselves or for their friends and families. It was able to defend itself with the help of its own network of highly committed personnel, by keeping a watchful eye on the milk unions, and frequently emphasizing the greater good of the farmers. A part of the NDDB's responsibility now is to keep politicians, bureaucrats, and multinational traders at a safe distance. To this end it has engaged itself in an incredibly shrewd guessing game of what the next move of the three will be and then forestalling them. But its continued success in such a strategy can never be fully assured. In fact there have been occasions when all the brain power and resources of the organization could not get it right, and it lost a few crucial rounds to the meddlesome trio of politicians, bureaucrats, and traders. As stated earlier, India's grassroots communities are still not democratically empowered enough to warn the elected and appointed public officials to keep their grabby disposition in check. Had they been ready to articulate and exercise their democratic right, the meddlesome trio would have been contained. As of now, that is not the case. Such an unpreparedness often emboldens the three with the hope that they might still be able to get away with their unfair advantages. Consequently, it is a scene of successive rounds of clashes with limited predictability, alternating with successes and failures.

In all this, the Indian judiciary has not been able to play a more effective role. In the winter of 1999, Prime Minister Vajpayee took the Indian judiciary to task for its tardiness in completing judicial work. But he could not add to the criticism by saying that the quality of judicial decisions, especially when powerful politicians, bureaucrats, or other interests are involved, left much to be desired. Such criticism would have amounted to an infraction on the autonomy of the judiciary and would have been disrespectful. But such a criticism could have come from the educated Indian middle class and professionals. Unfortunately, these two groups, so far, have a limited involvement in public issues. This leaves the print media, which, together with the electronic media, have done an admirable job of keeping the citizens informed. Consequently, the vital resource of any democracy, namely, the judiciary, remains untapped for furthering discussion on public interest and taking action.

In a country where both early capitalism and post-independence Nehruvian socialism have failed, and where liberalization is being brought in as a result of the poor performance of the state controlled economy and pressures from the international organizations, the NDDB's think tank has sought to guard its burgeoning cooperatives. It has tried to do this by educating its grassroots constituents with the help of various kinds of programs. Its spectacular performance is now a force to be reckoned with. In addition, it has breathed new life into grassroots institutions by pointing out that the participation of the poor, no matter how limited, will solicit response from rulers on a wide range of social and economic problems that concern them.

What needs to be explored further, nevertheless, is whether cooperatives can become the third sector in India's emerging political economy; a sector that can shelter the increasingly displaced recipients of welfare measures. As a greater measure of economic Darwinism makes headway into the Indian society and economy, those who cannot make it on their own will need a sector that can take advantage of their collective clout while working in the interest of all its members. And only a flourishing cooperative sector can do that. In short, the question is can it become a legatee of the shrinking welfare system in the acknowledgement that a substantial part of the Indian population, for a variety of reasons, cannot survive economically without assistance?

If this is the vision and ambition, then it will have to involve all those socially concerned individuals, who made the success of milk cooperatives possible. Such individuals would most likely come from the milk unions, the NDDB, self-effacing Gandhians, second generation Gandhians who embraced the non-violent militancy of JP, social and religious activists, retired professionals, repentant politicians, NGOs, academics, students, and just about anyone who thinks that he or she can make a difference. Together, they will supply a vast quantum of voluntary activity that will most certainly be needed. Add to this the gradually swelling crowd of expatriate returnees, who want to do something to help but do not know how, as an additional resource.

In the winter of 2000, the NDDB gave expression to its own notion of "Cooperative Democracy." Such an expression was given in the context of government interference and the need for autonomy on the part of cooperatives to experiment and develop on their own. The NDDB argued that in order to operate, expand, and serve their members as well as the general public, these grassroots cooperatives must have a space of their own that guarantees them freedom to get "a free flow of ideas" and experiment on them (NDDB 1999). Given the nature of governance in democratic India, where meddling bureaucrats and corrupt politicians have yet to be handed judicial reprimand and/or electoral defeat for their conduct, grassroots organizations and social activists have a long fight on their hands. They will, in the long run, win, but it will also take away a part of their attention, energy, and resources from their other urgent tasks.

Chapter 5

New Horizons

Most developing countries have waited a long time for a comprehensive solution to their problems; a solution that has not yet materialized. What has happened instead, in the more successful ones, is a pragmatic and context-effective use of whatever human and material resources have been available. Positive development has occurred through careful attention to social and economic priorities. Some countries have also benefited from international investment and favorable market forces. At the other extreme, there are countries where the government has squandered away the limited human and material resources causing its people to be victims of rigid ideologies, unsuitable imported solutions, or internal plutocracy.

In between these two extremes stands a third group of countries that have managed to effect some positive policy change after decades of limited achievement. Within this third group, there is an awareness of putting to use, or further use, whatever has already worked, given its peculiar development problems. India, at this stage of its development, falls in this third category of countries. The question remains whether its stunning success in the milk industry, by means of rural cooperatives, can be put to further use in related fields.

The principal organizers of the milk cooperatives, despite the achievement of making India the largest milk producer in the world in the short span of 50 years, have not fully turned their attention to areas beyond milk. That has given rise to a variety of speculation. International development personnel in New Delhi believe that efforts have not been made in other areas because of exhaustion after fighting corrupt politicians, power-hungry bureaucrats, and vested interests. Others believe there has been a need to remain focused on what has been successful, namely, milk. There are no guarantees that extending effort beyond the familiar terrain of milk within India's complex development process will succeed. So, many deem it prudent to stay with milk in order to continue to help the poor and the neglected of rural India. After all, these people comprise more than half of India's population.

While the technocrats in the NDDB had their own reasons for not venturing beyond the milk industry, they could not prevent some of the milk unions in different districts from experimenting with the possibility of going beyond milk in their own jurisdiction. Furthermore, at the grassroots level all across India, the success of the milk cooperatives convinced people that economic progress could be made in other areas. The demand for going beyond milk was periodically expressed. The social queue, which we identified in earlier chapters, expected the dairy organizers to solve other problems. Those at the base of the queue wanted more to be done by the cooperatives that were already in place. At that end the demand was for taking on more responsibility within the framework of existing institutions. At the top of the queue, the demand was for finding ways of helping them in their competitiveness to enter into different markets. Unlike those at the bottom of the queue they wanted another, more specialized, set of cooperative institutions to help them market their commercial crops such as sugarcane, cotton, edible oil seeds etc. The upper end producers were willing to take risks, but did not know how to go into those markets with a competitive edge. In other words, they wanted professional management and marketing skills, similar to what the network of milk cooperatives had offered. There was thus pressure from both ends of the social queue for the cooperatives to replicate their successful performance in related fields. While the people at the lower end waited patiently, as they had no other alternative, those at the upper end were restless and often went in search of solutions on their own. While they were experimenting with alternatives, they were also vocal in their criticism of the milk only policy.

166

In the meanwhile, under duress from the central and state governments, the organizers of the NDDB started to extend efforts beyond milk, by instituting cooperatives for edible oil seeds, trees, salt, and, in select regions, fruits and vegetables. Often, however, these were undertaken *ad hoc* or without regard to wider application. This was in contrast to the thoroughness evinced in the milk cooperatives.

While the NDDB persisted with its formally stated milk only policy, it experimented, albeit less enthusiastically, with other agricultural crops for possible cooperatization in the future. While the NDDB did not hold open discussions with the milk unions on this topic, there was no attempt to discourage the unions from trying out whatever they wanted in their own jurisdiction. Only occasionally was there a word of caution for them. The discussion on going beyond milk did not flourish for the simple reason that milk itself was such a gigantic undertaking in the huge subcontinent of India. Everyone was connected to the industry. Despite a quarter of a century's ceaseless effort, the NDDB had been able to cover only half the total number of districts in the country by the start of the new millennium. To stay with milk, therefore, did not require any private or public justification. Consequently, extending cooperative dairying to the remaining districts of India remained its prime concern. Most of the experiments in going beyond milk were thus left to the milk unions. There was tacit approval of "beyond milk" policy in those unions that had registered success in increasing their milk productivity. Indeed no one could argue against their success.

Most of the thinking and planning for the future of cooperative dairying was done at the NDDB headquarters in Anand. Its resources, and an "all-India" perspective, together with highly trained personnel known for their integrity and speed to put new proposals in place, often overwhelmed the milk unions. Nevertheless, some of the unions did try to go beyond milk as a logical follow-up to their success with the milk industry. The assumption was that success in milk meant a good possibility of success in related fields. The union pressure on the NDDB to extend its efforts came mostly in the form of suggestions. Primarily, unions were left to pursue their own methods of exploring other areas provided milk remained their primary concern.

But underneath all that the NDDB itself had not fully grasped the force and nature of the rural dynamics it had unleashed. At the grassroots level, it had literally built new economic communities out of a fractured rural society in India: fractured along the lines of caste, religion, and class. Throughout India, the residents of most villages rarely formed an enduring community. Periodically, they came together over issues that agitated them and then went their separate ways. In the villages with milk cooperatives, however, something miraculous had happened: the cooperatives had become the center not only of community life, but also of development efforts in general. And as the lower strata had been inducted into the community, sharing power with the upper, it became truly representative of grassroots social realities. Often given to self-effacement, even the unions did not fully appreciate what they had achieved. They wanted to remain focused on milk as their primary goal, but simultaneously pay attention to what else could be done.

So much was being done at the milk union level that the NDDB had to appoint research teams to find out what was happening. Being at the grassroots level themselves, the union staff experienced the producers' readiness to advance into fields such as agriculture, health, hygiene, education, public participation, and the social and economic mobility of the traditionally disadvantaged among them, including the tribals, ex-untouchables, women, and so on. More recently, micro-savings groups had generated sufficient liquidity requiring direction for investment. The demand from those communities was that since the milk cooperatives were highly successful in reaching out to the majority of its members, similar institutions should be set up to address the other economic and social problems of the community. Their preference, therefore, was for a set of parallel cooperative institutions.

To this was added the voice of social activists and socially concerned dairymen to explore the possibility of venturing beyond milk. Suddenly the milk cooperatives had become context-effective tools for bringing together untapped resources: economic, human, managerial, and technical. Such resources had already given India a world-class network of cooperative dairies. Why not further use these resources, or combine them in new ways? Such combination might produce yet another success story.

But the NDDB had its own reasons for being less enthusiastic. For one thing, its struggle against meddlesome bureaucrats, corrupt politicians, and profit hungry traders in milk economy was not yet over. Much remained to be accomplished in that field alone. With great difficulty the NDDB was able to register success against these three pillars of corruption in India. New ventures would most likely mean new battles against corruption and, indeed, there were no guarantees of success. While that convinced the NDDB to remain cautious, the same could not be said for the successful milk unions that wanted to go beyond milk. In addition, the unions had youthful energy, vision, and the willingness to get a bad name for a good cause if needed. There was nothing to hold them back. The new generation of milk technocrats in successful milk unions wanted to attempt other projects within their own jurisdiction. They were even talking in terms of making use of the opportunities provided by liberalization and globalization.

Indeed, it was true that the milk cooperatives, by virtue of their enormous success, had already come to acquire significance in areas beyond milk, and of this the younger generation of tech-nocrats, managers, and grassroots personnel were fully aware. Whenever these unions got a sympathetic chairman and board, their hopes for going beyond milk were roused. The same was true of the milk producers in successful unions. They, too, were looking for relief or progress in other compartments of agricultural life for themselves and their families. For the first time in rural India, an institution that they had voluntarily joined had registered enormous success. Now the wisest thing the milk producers could do was to latch on to milk cooperatives in order to solve their other problems.

If milk cooperatives could be used to eliminate the middlemen in the industry and provide better returns, could similar institutions accomplish the same thing in vegetables and other crops? Furthermore, cannot the milk cooperatives help milk producers obtain human healthcare services that are as efficient as their veterinary services? Then there is the question of educating children. The village schools run by the state were not always efficient, and sometimes the teachers did not even show up. The cooperative institutions in villages were expected to find a solution for education. Finally, cooperative institutions were also expected to find a solution for helping "backward" communities and women. In short, once the cooperatives succeeded in one field, there was no end to increasing demands on them to get involved in the other problems of rural dwellers.

In this chapter we will examine these and other related issues under the following subsections: (I) Some Early Experiences; (II) Bold Regional Experiments; (III) Coordinates of Going Beyond Milk; and finally (IV) New Horizons. We will now examine each of these in some details.

I. Some Early Experiences

In the early days of Amul Dairy the organizers of the milk cooperatives in Anand were quite receptive to the idea of going beyond milk. In fact, milk was considered to be the most difficult product to bring into a cooperative framework because of the logistical problems involved in collecting, processing, and marketing a highly perishable commodity. Unlike milk, other agricultural products such as rice, sugarcane, and lemon were considered easier pursuits under the cooperative framework. There was, however, one essential difference and that is in the production of milk, a large number of small and marginal farmers were involved. Their limited resources permitted them to invest in small numbers of animals consisting of buffalo and /or cows and get a better price for milk than the one that was offered to them by milk traders. Consequently, the moral appeal of helping the farmers out was always there for dairy organizers despite the logistical problems involved. Having brought the small and marginal farmers together in a cooperative situation, there was the theoretical possibility of moving on to other agricultural products. Accordingly, during the decade of 1960s, Amul Dairy had toyed with the idea of building cooperatives for rice, sugar, lemon, etc. Such an exercise was likely to bring Amul in conflict with large farmers and traders without helping the small ones. Moreover, large farmers with deep pockets were likely to influence the market. Consequently, wisdom demanded that it restrict itself to milk.

But it was not always easy to stay away from other agricultural commodities. Kurien's success in building milk cooperatives brought pressure on him to make similar attempts in other agricultural commodities. In order to protect milk cooperatives from politicians and bureaucrats, he had to cultivate good relations with the top brass of Indian politics, including successive prime ministers. Practically all the prime ministers of India, from Jawaharlal Nehru and Lalbahdur Shastri onwards, visited Amul Dairy and the NDDB. They wanted to have a first-hand idea of how he was helping small farmers. They were extremely pleased with what Kurien had achieved. They had also given him direct access to the Prime Minister's office, should problems arise. Simultaneously, both Amul and the NDDB had become symbols of what India was trying to do for its poor. World-class leaders visited Amul and were pleasantly surprised to see all that had been achieved. By the1980s it had a cluster of institutions that had world-class scientists, engineers, managers, veterinarians, and dairy technologists in them. This deeply impressed the visitors. We had the privilege of talking to many of those visitors in various guesthouses. Almost every visitor came out with an expression of wonder accompanied by praise that India could achieve such technological and managerial sophistication and also devise highly practical institutions that could work in rural India.

The top political brass in New Delhi, nevertheless, extracted a price from Kurien for having protected him from obstructionist bureaucrats, mostly in the Ministry of Agriculture. He was to build cooperatives for edible oil seeds growers, salt makers, and tree growers, none of which would do as well as milk. But he had no other alternative but to make his staff at the NDDB do their best. If Indira Gandhi could not get a good price for the tomatoes grown in her garden, Kurien had to build vegetable growers' cooperatives in a few major cities of India in order to keep the promise that he made to her. His direct access to them was very important to protect his vast network of milk cooperatives. Thus, cooperatives in areas other than milk were a kind of a price he had to pay to protect the cooperatives for milk. After that he did not want to go beyond milk on his own. He wanted to stay with what he and his team at the NDDB were good at. Besides, even in milk there was much yet to be accomplished. Greedy politicians, some of them in league with vested interests, and opinionated bureaucrats, had slowed him down. In every state he had to fight his way through despite his assurances to them that he would bear all the losses and let the states that joined him keep all the profits.

His fight against them was a lonely fight. There was hardly anyone at the state level to support him. The print media in India, which has been a pillar of its democracy, did not take the rural development problems seriously. Political parties did not take up the cause of milk cooperatives because there were no promises of votes in them. Some left-wing intellectuals saw the cooperatives as an archaic way of helping the poor. Others waited for Western intellectuals to certify that something worthwhile was happening there and, therefore, deserved their support. Many men and women had just become used to not bothering about what was happening at the grassroots level. They already had so many other things to worry about. Ironically, however, these same men and women were very proud that every morning these farmer-owned and operated organizations delivered good quality milk and milk products at their doorsteps. It was parallel to Indian democracy; everyone was very proud that, despite great shortcomings, India had the world's largest democracy. But apart from the professional political class, very few of its educated men and women wanted to help it overcome its deficiencies. The urban educated often did not even bother to vote in big numbers.

Most of the explorations in building cooperatives beyond milk were conducted by the NDDB-appointed technocrats or the younger generation of milk union leaders with substantial experience of working with the NDDB. They undertook such explorations either after their apprenticeship at the apex body or while they were assigned to different states. Those technocrats, administrators, veterinarians, and marketing experts understood the changing social reality at the grassroots level after the milk cooperatives had been in place for a few years. Social activists of various regions also assisted most of these bold explorers. We have already referred to their fruitful combination.

Cooperative dairying, by virtue of its tremendous success in rural India, had acquired significance for a wide range of agricultural products. This was because, barring the Green Revolution in Indian agriculture whereby the country was not only able to feed its growing population but also able to export food grains, vegetables, fruits, fruit juices, flowers, etc., nothing else had achieved so much in rural India.

The milk cooperatives had not only succeeded in improving the economic condition of the lower strata of Indian society, but had also earned the respect and gratitude of urban dwellers through the high quality milk and milk products. If urban India demanded baby food, ice cream, cheese, chocolate etc., this network of milk cooperatives was there to provide these products for them. It even went into the field of edible oil, bottled mineral water, pizza, and so on, to meet the growing demand of urban Indians. And all of the products were trusted for their quality.

All along, while experimenting with these new products, the principal organizers did not want to go beyond milk. Their hesitation was understandable. For one thing there was the fear that the responsibility for new undertakings might dilute their effort. And therefore, in the end they might not enjoy the same reputation for quality and service. While the top organizers agonized over how much to expand into other areas, at heart they also remained committed to the ideal of eliminating the middleman from almost all areas of agricultural products. In his address during the 50th anniversary of Amul Dairy, Kurien himself gave expression to those sentiments:

> There are more than 80,000 Anand Pattern cooperatives in our country, owned by some 1 crore members [ten million, 1997]. As pleased as we are with that achievement, it is far from enough. We need cooperatives dealing with every commodity and in every village in our nation. We need genuine cooperatives, owned and controlled by their members and managed by real professionals. To achieve this we need new cooperative laws, laws that are enabling not prescriptive; laws that leave to the members the decisions that affect the resources they produce; laws that do not protect wrong-doers; laws that do not allow political interest to hijack a business that is serving people regardless of language, religion, caste or political affiliation. (Kurien 1996:xiv-xv)

Kurien's words clearly revealed his frustration with the existing cooperative laws, which allowed politicians and administrators to interfere with the normal working of cooperatives. The corollary of this, for Kurien, was that if there were more cooperative institutions without adequate laws, then the extent of interference by politicians and bureaucrats, to serve their own interests, would be that much greater. So, restrict the NDDB's scope to milk, and get by with *ad hoc* policies whenever new responsibilities are pushed on its shoulders.

The extension from milk, therefore, had to be a temporary measure. While structures established for commodities other than milk had a sound institutional base, much more could have been done if only the political interference in determining them was not there, or if sound cooperative laws had been in place.

While such concerns were publicly aired, the NDDB achieved the impossible. As stated earlier, it was able to build new economic communities out of fractured rural societies. That had rarely happened in India's long history. At the best of times Indians had lived in highly stratified arrangements of caste and religion, inter-acting with each other only during rare social and interpersonal occasions. If there was any one country where *community life* was markedly absent, excepting on rare social occasions or political agitations, it was India. Having lived in fractured societies, the people associated with the NDDB did not realize that around grass-roots cooperative institutions they had, in fact, brought the entire milk producing community together in every village. But that the rare happening of coming together could have been used in order to go beyond milk was not clear to everyone. Milk pouring, can-carry-ing, rural dwellers had now accomplished, under a cooperative umbrella, what the countless saints and sages of India had failed to do. They had come together across the intractable boundaries of caste and religion, and had also economically benefited themselves in the process.

Their entire rural universe was opening up to new ideas, initia-tives, and possibilities. And what is more, the NDDB's 750 (2004 figure) highly skilled, dedicated, result-conscious and corruption-free employees were there to work with them and for them. In Anand they had to be held back from venturing into something unrelated to milk, but in the district unions they had much greater freedom to explore new possibilities along with the unions' tech-nocrats. Some of them, as we shall see, did precisely that, and with remarkable results.

II.   Bold Regional Experiments

In this section we will briefly examine the various experiments undertaken by the milk unions, often with the support of NDDB technocrats and the involvement of social activists. Not all experiments succeeded, but those that did also spawned a highly efficient and dedicated local leadership. Here are a few examples.

Consumers' Cooperatives: A Non-Starter

In different parts of rural India, we were repeatedly asked the question: "why don't the unions and the NDDB help us build consumers' cooperatives that could operate side-by-side with, and in the same building as, the milk cooperatives?" This question was asked no matter where we went in the country. And we had no answer. Sometimes, in order to ward off the question, we just said that they, i.e., the milk unions and/or the NDDB, expected the local community to take the initiative and organize them.

The reasons for creating milk cooperatives, to begin with, was to eliminate middlemen and to help milk producers get the maximum returns on their milk. A similar rationale was there for having consumers' cooperatives. While milk cooperatives saved milk producers from some middlemen, they did nothing to save them from the middlemen in the market who sucked back all their earnings from milk. Why was the middleman *per se* not targeted? In question here was the very presence of middleman, not just in the milk trade but in all other economic activities that touched the lives of rural dwellers. Again, we had no answer to that except to say that the milk cooperative organizations might not want the additional responsibility.

In the search for another answer, we confronted a very senior official with our personal experiences in price differences at various shops in a village and elsewhere. The prices of vegetables, sugar, tea, soap, and matches were usually the highest from vendors with pushcarts that were parked beside the milk cooperative buildings.

And they came in big numbers, especially on payday. Next highest in price were the village shopkeepers on street corners. The lowest prices were found in the market towns at a distance of three to five kilometers outside of the village. An article that was Rs.10 in the market town would cost Rs.12 in the village grocery stores, and Rs.15 at the pushcart vendors conveniently parked outside the cooperative building. On paydays, especially, euphoric women, with a bundle of currency notes in their hands, wanted to carry something home for the family and they often bought from the pushcarts. We narrated that experience to the senior official in Amul Dairy, whose response to us was: "What can we do? We just do not want to get involved in consumer coop business!"

It was understandable that milk cooperatives did not want to spread themselves too thin into diverse undertakings. They wanted to stay with what they were good at, which, after all had been a Herculean struggle against all odds. They had identified the various needs of rural dwellers and strictly concentrated on the most important one: their livelihood. The idea was to secure the best possible returns on milk for the producers and then let them be the judge of where to spend their money.

In the absence of direction from the top organizers, those regions where social workers were active and/or grassroots communities themselves had provided dynamic leaders, consumer cooperatives were started; and these were few and far between. They also lacked professionalism and market savvy. Union and NDDB resources in both categories would have made a big difference. Consequently, outside milk the greedy middlemen prevailed.

As stated earlier, Father Berechi of Surat-Bharuch district understood the problem and asked the registrar of cooperatives to give him permission to organize a consumers' cooperative. Nearly two years had passed and the registrar had not acted on his request. The registrar did not want to annoy the local shopkeepers by giving permission to start a consumers' cooperative in Berechi's village called Nivalda.

Explorations into Health Services

One of the most useful non-milk services set up by a dairy organization was in the field of human health: the T.K. Foundation,
established by Amul Dairy. This was considered extensively in an
earlier chapter. So here we will provide only a brief summary with
a little background information. An average Indian village often has
one or two certified private medical practitioners, uncertified practitioners of traditional medicine, and visiting medical personnel
maintained by district and state bodies. The private practitioners
diagnose and dispense medicine at a considerable cost so that only
the more affluent people can afford them. Since traditional medicines often take too long to cure, villagers need medical help similar
to the kind enjoyed by people of affluence. And as far as the state
maintained medical staff is concerned, it is invariably wasteful,
often dysfunctional, and fails to perform the most routine duties.
Repeatedly we heard from villagers that their animals receive better
care than members of their family. Across the country comparisons
were made between the efficient animal health services at the hands
of union veterinarians, and the irregular or even non-existent health
services for humans.

For a long time Amul did not want to face the problem of
making health services available to milk producers in the district.
Amul often told the villagers that they should ask the state to
provide health services for them. It also knew that nothing would
come of these requests. It should be noted that Amul could have
taken a little bit longer before getting involved, as there were no
riots or overt demonstrations for health care. But the mounting criticism affected the socially concerned individuals. It must be said to
the credit of Kurien, and his colleague Dalaya, that they agreed to
try out something different that would deliver health care to the milk
producers of the district. They also appointed sympathetic individuals to prepare a report on it with practical proposals that could be
implemented.

As stated earlier, the costs of running the newly established rural health service under Tribhuvandas Foundation, were shared by the Foundation, Amul Dairy, and the cooperative members at the village level. Interestingly enough, Amul's cost was about 1 percent of its annual receipts from the sale of milk. The cost for a cooperative member (and his/her family per year was Rs.25 (U.S.$0.50 approximately). By the year 2000, a team of village level health workers, roving nurses, and doctors at the headquarters were providing healthcare services to more than 600 villages in the district. The Foundation had thus put in place a cost-efficient health linkage that was unknown to rural India.

So great was the success of this health scheme that it was highly acclaimed by scholars, international development agencies, and various health foundations in India and abroad. However, it could not help incurring the wrath of the non-functioning health bureaucracy of Gujarat state. Initially, all kinds of obstacles were put in its way. Finally, the politicians of the state, in order not to annoy the rural public, started supporting the activities of the Foundation. In the mid-1990s, the state government even sought its help to launch family planning services in the district.

Since nearly 80 percent of births in rural India take place at the hands of *dais* or birth attendants, the state government wanted them to be trained by the Foundation in maintaining the standard of hygiene. Later, it even gave a contract to the Foundation to prepare kits for the birth attendants to use while attending to their work of helping pregnant women deliver babies.

Unfortunately, the Foundation's work was seen by some as an additional burden on the milk producers of the district. It was also perceived as saving the state government from the problematic situation of being unable to provide medical services for which it had collected taxes. Most of the money earmarked for rural health was spent on the payroll and travel allowances of bureaucrats, and for buying equipment and medicine, which were never fully used. Sometimes such funds were diverted to other wasteful expenses in the district. Since the rural citizenry had never fully organized to hold the government accountable for the way taxpayers' money was spent, those who had squandered the funds had nothing to fear.

Amul and the NDDB went through an agonizing internal debate on what to do when some of the highly developed dairy organizations thought of introducing similar health schemes in their own regions. The word from the NDDB was that the Tribhuvandas Foundation health scheme was "unreplicable," and they cautioned other dairies from embarking on similar projects. Such a decision was not to be taken lightly. The NDDB, in particular, knew of the dire need for health services in rural areas, having set a standard of its own as far as animal health was concerned. Its rationale was that the state governments would exploit the milk cooperatives for more and more functions for which they had collected taxes and squandered them away on corrupt practices and schemes. A similar urgency existed in matters of primary education, drinking water, sanitation, roads, housing, street lighting and so on. If the inefficient administration was "bailed out" in one area, there is no knowing what it would expect next.

Dudhsagar of Mehsana, which has now excelled Amul in milk collection, and in quality of service to its members, came close to emulating Amul on a similar health service. It even established what was called the "Sagar Foundation" but refrained from taking the ultimate step of implementing a rural health network. Consequently, Amul Dairy was alone in going beyond milk to rural health.

Uncoordinated Efforts in Cattle Improvement

From the start, the NDDB put enormous emphasis on improving the cattle breed. For that purpose, it had to wage a battle against powerful politicians who had their own pet local breeds. For example, the redoubtable former prime minister of India, Morarji Desai, who had taken a keen interest in the growth of the milk cooperatives in Gujarat since before Indian independence, was a great admirer of the *kankrej* cow, a famed milch animal that belonged to the district of Banas. This breed, which was once known for its extraordinarily graceful looks and high milk yield, had deteriorated over the years for want of proper breeding management. For years, bulls with a doubtful pedigree sired the female calves. Kankrej cows, therefore, could not become the mainstay of dairying unless, through proper management, they could be restored to their full milk producing capacity. But the strong-willed Morarji Desai, who understood little about dairying, insisted that kankarej cows should become the mainstay of dairying regardless of their milk yielding capacity. The venerated politician had to be convinced that buffalo had a relatively greater milk yield and were also owned by the bulk of milk producers. Cooperatives had to be built on the existing animal resources of the region and, from there, seek to gradually improve the milk giving capacity of those animals. For years, Morarji Desai remained a strong lobbyist for the animal he loved so dearly without realizing that the kankrej cow had to improve in its milk giving capacity before it could become an animal of the rural masses.

The NDDB consistently encouraged research to improve indigenous animals. It imported Holstein-Friesian semen from Western countries to produce an indigenous crossbred cow with high milk yield. It also produced vaccines to prevent diseases that plagued the indigenous and crossbred animals alike. What it could not do, however, was make it mandatory for every milk union to engage in research in improving different varieties of regional breeds. And in India, there are a wide variety of such breeds. This task was left to the milk unions. If some unions were engaged in doing research, they received research grants and encouragement from the NDDB. One such union, which was actively engaged in research, was Dudhsagar.

Quite coincidentally, Dudhsagar happened to employ Dr. A.S. Dave, a brilliant and dedicated veterinarian who combined his research interests with close contact with grassroots communities and their problems relating to the improvement of the milk yielding capacity of the animals. The district of Mehsana already had two incomparable resources: a good breed of local buffalo called *mesani,* and the women of Chaudhury, an agriculturist caste who had earned a reputation for having developed the mesani to its fullest potential. Dudhsagar Dairy, under Dave's leadership, both in research and its application at the grassroots level, brought to bear the usefulness of animal science and social conscience which were not known before. In a span of nearly three decades, he and his men transformed the character of the milk giving animal, both buffalo and cross-bred cow, in the district and made Dudhsagar the premier dairy of India overtaking Amul, the flagship of dairying. While in other milk unions it was difficult to persuade milk bureaucracy to keep close contact with villages, Dave and his men were hard to find at the desk even when some important papers needed their attention. They were almost all the time in villages. They thus went *beyond* milk to who all they could help in making them effective milk producers.

This required not only painstaking laboratory work in the most professional manner, but also meticulous observation of the various cowsheds in villages for a realistic assessment of changes at the ground level. Veterinary researchers developed close relationships with the average cowshed owner in order to understand the entire situation. It did not take very long to convince the villagers that the entire exercise was for *their* benefit. Also, the women who managed the animals in cowsheds worked closely with research-minded veterinarians who were now going beyond animal health to consider productivity. The vets also concentrated on the possibility of bringing the animals into pregnancy and lactation at an earlier age than was thought possible. This enhanced the milk giving capacity of the animals and therefore improved returns on the farmers' investments.

Further, influenced by their social conscience, Dr. Dave and his team made a decision to consider and help the poor of the village who owned poor quality animals. While the relatively well-to-do producers could replace their animals, the poor, with their limited investment, were stuck with the animals they had. Consequently, despite a highly competitive atmosphere in the village, these men did rounds in the poorer localities of the village. They even gave, free of charge, female calves brought from the Jagudan Farm to the lower strata of village society. Under Dave's leadership, Dudhsagar employed keen insight into animal science research and social consciousness in order to improve village conditions at many levels. In a span of nearly three decades, he and his men transformed the character of the milk giving animal, both buffalo and crossbred cow, and made Dudhsagar the premier dairy of India, overtaking Amul, the flagship of dairying. While in other milk unions it was difficult to persuade the milk bureaucracy to keep close contact with villages, Dave and his men, on the other hand, spent the majority of their time in the villages. Indeed, they did all they could to make the rural poor effective milk producers.

Dudhsagar encountered its own share of jealousy and resent-ment. Initially, the dairy community did not believe everything that had been achieved. When the figures of milk productivity and procurement began to appear in annual reports, there was mild praise and respect merely for the increased quantity of milk. The milk unions, often deeply engrossed in their own problems, were slow to grasp completely the significance of the qualitative work that Dudhasagar was doing apart from collecting more milk. The increased quantity of milk was even rationalized as the product of superior animals of the region, such as the mesani, rather than as the result of the improvements that the veterinarians had instituted. As far as the quality of their work was concerned, we often had to convince people in other unions of the *significance* of what had been achieved. By and large, therefore, Dudhsagar's achievement was rarely examined as possible inspiration for new policies for other milk unions.

Advancement of the Poor and the Disadvantaged

Within cooperative institutions, some of the boldest experiments for going beyond milk came from the South Gujarat milk unions of Sumul and Valsad. As we saw in earlier chapters, both were the outgrowths of the broader social and political movement in which Mahatma Gandhi was involved. After his salt *Satyagraha* in this region, Gandhi started his constructive program. He knew that his agitation against the mighty colonial rule would have to be launched again and again, but between such agitations he wanted his followers to keep themselves busy with the various assignments prescribed in his constructive program; one of which was to do social work in areas inhabited by the poor and the deprived, including the Dalits (he called them *Harijans*). One way of helping them was to concentrate on their problems of illiteracy, lack of hygiene, liquor consumption, and economic destitution. In rural areas in particular, this meant doing something for the small farmers and the landless. Through his emphasis on constructive work, Gandhi had thus prepared a generation of social workers to take interest in cooperatives in various fields.

Ironically, the rich farmers of South Gujarat were the first to benefit from Gandhi's teachings. They built cooperatives of all kinds to protect their interests in textiles, cotton, and sugar. Only when the milk cooperatives arrived in this region, was it possible to bring in the poor and very poor under the cooperative umbrella.

Together, the Gandhians and JPians in the region united in common cause against the vested interests in numerous sectors of the economy. Ironically, the vested interests also enjoyed the protection of Congressmen who pretended to be inspired by socialist ideology. The JPians and Gandhians built a forest workers union to protect the tribals, ran small scale industries, supported educational institutions, gave a helping hand to the famous *Lijjat Papad* factory that gave part-time employment to nearly one thousand women, and gave substantial support to the milk cooperatives. They were of inestimable value to Sumul Dairy when Sumul attempted to get involved in the tribal areas.

As discussed earlier, the milk unions of Sumul and Valsad are based in the tribal belt of their respective districts. So deep was their penetration into those districts that nearly 80 percent of their milk collection came from these tribal areas. Although the milk cooperatives went there primarily to collect milk, their very entry into the region began to change their outlook. For one thing, it is difficult to go into tribal villages and concentrate solely on collecting milk. In those villages, a broad range of problems immediately became evident. And while the tribal villages began to change under the impact of cooperatives, the policies of these two unions towards them came to acquire a broader social character, seeking to help in areas other than, or in addition to, milk. A similar change took place in the attitude of the Christian missionaries working in Surat and Bharuch districts. They turned from their narrow religious goals to focusing on economic advancement, education, health, and the social development of the tribals in general. The point we are trying to make here is that the very nature of social activism of all those involved in the enterprise of building milk cooperatives changed, regardless of their initial entry as milk technocrats, Gandhians or JPians, or Jesuit preachers.

III.   The Coordinates of Going Beyond Milk

Our observations of milk unions over the years suggested that whenever the following four factors are present, simultaneously or sequentially, there is potential for development beyond milk: socially concerned milk technocrats; a tradition of social activism in the region; the emergence of grassroots leaders; and an accelerated demand for milk.

In the case of the two premier milk cooperatives, namely, Amul and Dudhsagar, all four factors were present. Technical personnel like Kurien in Amul and B.C. Bhatt in Dudhsagar were two of the finest examples of socially concerned technocrats. Likewise T.K. Patel in Amul and Motibhai Chaudhury in Dudhsagar represented the best in the continuing tradition of social activism, which came through the Indian national movement. In both of their districts, there was no dearth of grassroots leaders. These dairies were able to meet the demand for milk both locally and nationally.

The socially concerned technocrats of the latter day Sumul and Vasudhara milk unions developed a vision and a strategy for *deliberately* going beyond milk. In both of them the four factors herein outlined were also present.

The burgeoning economy of Surat district placed an increasing amount of disposable income in the hands of its residents, a substantial part of which was meant for food, including milk and milk products. As a result, from the 1960s to the 1990s, Surat was perpetually short of milk. No matter how much milk was procured, it was not enough for Surat. This high demand led Sumul's veterinary staff to build milk cooperatives in its tribal communities. In that endeavor it had a remarkable success. When social activists, either religious or secular, worked with them, grassroots leadership increased in a number of villages. Such leadership enabled Sumul to develop in areas other than the milk industry. It was thus a two-way movement; Sumul built grassroots tribal communities, and the communities, in turn, facilitated the implementation of its programs and policies for going beyond milk.

Sumul's excursion into the tribal region to procure more milk went beyond the conventional approach to dairying. It gambled on converting India's most backward social segment into milk producers when they did not even seem to have the necessary resources. It was, in fact, one of the greatest triumphs in cooperative dairying in India. Sumul could easily have imported milk from neighboring districts, which had a surplus and sold it locally. Instead, it converted the tribals into milk producers and who then met the insatiable demand of urban dwellers. In so doing, Sumul thus evinced that dairying could be used to pull people out of poverty.

Vasudhara took this a step further. Vasudhara concentrated on its women to stabilize its development; this in a district where more than 50 percent of the population is comprised of tribals.

For a number of years, Valsad district poured its milk into Sumul. When it became a separate milk union, the question facing its socially concerned staff was how could it be unique within the family of milk cooperatives of India? The staff did not have to look far for the answer. In tribal society, women play an important part. Why not employ women to build the milk cooperatives? Like Sumul's gamble with the tribals, Vasudhara's gamble with their women paid off. By the year 2000, more than 60 percent of its milk cooperatives were entirely run by women. The apex body in Anand, namely, the NDDB, according to Vasudhara milk technocrats, thought that Valsad was too progressive and might have to change its course. But those fears proved to be unfounded. In the winter of the year 2000, other milk unions from the rest of India were asking Valsad for insight into its significant achievements.

Neither Surat nor Valsad rested on these early successes. Fortunately, for them, the four preconditions of going beyond milk, which we stated earlier, were present to support their effort and enable them to continue with various kinds of social development.

Sumul's managing director, P.R. Patel, gave us a glimpse of his vision, now that his milk union had been a resounding success not only in quantity but also in the quality of its work among the poor of the district. Patel represented a new generation of milk technocrats. For him, since the new policy of India was for the liberalization of the economy, why not benefit from that liberalization with regard to the milk cooperatives. No use fighting the tide of liberalization. Patel combined vision with commonsense. Money from milk would go into agriculture, enabling the grassroots communities to grow fruits and vegetables. Patel anticipated that the milk unions could help organize cooperatives in other fields. Of course milk would always be the first priority, but now some additional responsibilities could be shouldered by the cooperative structure.

The question for Patel, therefore, was whether fruit and vegetable cooperatives could provide significant returns. On milk, Sumul claimed to have returned a staggering 85 percent of the sale price to producer. This was largely because Surat's population needed pasteurized milk rather than milk products, and the margin of profit on the former was often higher. If Patel is able to do a similar thing in fruits and vegetables, in a few years' time his district will end up as the richest district in the country, despite its overwhelming tribal population.

Patel said that the milk cooperatives were imposing limits on themselves when they confined themselves to milk only. One of the areas he wants to explore is the possibility of a centrally located *biogas* plant in every village where there is a milk cooperative. Owners of animals are not maximizing the potential benefits of cow dung. This is because there is no organization to guide them on what is possible. If a corresponding cooperative structure were to develop, with the state-of-the-art technology in biogas, all the villages in the district could solve their problems concerning fuel and lighting. Many benefits would come from the establishment of such organizations.

While Surat was still at the conceptual stage, Valsad was putting into practice policies and projects designed to develop other industries without undermining the success of the milk industry. Having built women-run milk cooperatives in the majority of the villages in the district, Valsad did not want to limit these women to the confines of milk cooperatives. The women of Valsad had the energy, enthusiasm, and resources. Their success in bringing in substantial income from milk for their families, in less than a decade, had made them believe in their ability to do bigger and better things. Since they occupied a lower position in the India's social hierarchy, the corresponding effect on their morale was that much greater. With the help of Valsad's dedicated union organizers, the women were confident they would rise to greater social and economic heights.

Vashibhai, the deeply committed managing director of Vasudhara, and his staff consisting of Suresh Desai, Bina Desai, and others, did not have much of a family life. They were at the milk union office seven days a week and at odd hours. They were constantly planning for, and anticipating, social and economic developments. Vashibhai's vision, as already stated, was to set the tribal women free with the help of two or three high-yielding crossbred cows. One way to achieve this was to get his own staff deeply involved in directing them toward building their cow herd with the help of subsidies and loans, and also savings from the sale of milk. Unlike Surat's managing director, Vashibhai wanted to pay attention to family's need for energy coming from biogas as an individual undertaking in its own backyard. In this project, various foundries in the district were helpful. They designed biogas plants that could utilize not only animal dung, but also human waste from the latrines. The two waste pipes were combined into a "Y," one coming from the family toilet and the other from the cowshed, which then became a source of raw material for the biogas plant. In the shortest possible time, they got a large number of households to accept the proposal. With the help of tubes provided by the local manufacturers, biogas became available for the family stove, for a few hours every day, and also for lighting at night. For the average tribal home, this constituted additional savings.

The union was instrumental in helping women organize their own micro-credit groups in village after village. Although the amount saved per month was from Rs.20 to Rs.100 (less than U.S.$.50 to $3) per household, each village had a surplus saving of about Rs.2 lakhs (U.S.$4,444) waiting to be invested. As stated earlier, the movement of micro saving and lending may solve a part of the rural credit problem where banks are not very helpful.

Vashibahi and his colleagues do not want to stop there. They also want to focus on health and, possibly, education.

In this connection, one of the things to remember is that the earlier milk producers of various unions came from the middle and higher rungs of rural society. They wanted to treat milk cooperatives as institutions that were strictly concerned with milk. This was so despite the *Choryasi Taluka Cooperative* in Surat, which became a part of Sumul, but did not confine itself to milk. Both in Kheda and Mehsana, the thinking was to stay with milk. However, the tribals and the social activists of Sumul and Vasudhara changed this. With the overwhelming population of tribals in the district also came the need to push the milk cooperatives to other uses. The same was true in Rajasthan and Bihar.

The demand was not for a fundamental shift in the focus of milk cooperatives. Given their limitations, poorer communities tend to approach their problems more holistically. Whatever can help should be pressed into service. For them, the policy of "milk only" was an arbitrary, self-imposed limitation on the cooperatives. Since there is hardly any other organization in rural India that has done so much for the advancement of the poor, the cooperatives ought not to be asked to stop at milk.

In this game of going beyond milk, Surat has had an advantage of nearly two decades over Valsad. When Valsad finally came to have its own milk union under the title of Vasudhara, Surat had already taken the important step of going beyond milk by building milk producers from among its tribal population. And when Vasudhara came on stream as a young milk union, what Surat had achieved was also a part of its heritage because earlier it was a part of Sumul. While it was relatively easy for Vasudhara to move into the field of building milk cooperatives for tribal women, what it could not do, because of the time factor, is build grassroots leadership in those villages to work and develop on their own. In the district of Surat, given the additional advantage of the heritage of South Gujarat's social activism, there are many villages with grassroots leadership, which sometimes even goes beyond Sumul itself. And that was evident in the villages of Anaval, Nivalda, Mandal, and Gantoli. These villages experimented with, as we saw, eduation, conumer coops, and health and hygiene. For Vasudhara, that kind of leadership is still a few years away. Nevertheless, the leadership that we observed in Railia Falia had women so confident, they believed they could build micro credit groups that would one day emerge as a rural bank. Given the depth of commitment and dedication of Vasudhara's staff, this may happen. Already they are in the forefront of the women's cooperative movement in India.

It is remarkable that the grassroots communities in these districts, with their additional income from milk, have not diluted their social goals that lie beyond milk. There is now a perception that they can achieve social and economic goals that are as important to them and their families as is milk, provided they have the help of the milk unions. In their part of the world, the Patidars and Desais, who have better tracts of land, have often achieved their social and economic goals through their individual effort. Coming from behind, given India's deeply rooted hierarchical structure, they too, through the cooperative structure, can achieve some social and economic goals, which are very important to them and their families. Initially, it will have to be a collective effort, through cooperatives, with the possibility of individuated efforts to follow.

This generation of adivasis will, no doubt, have their own limitations. After all, only a few years ago, they, along with their wives and children worked as *majoors.* They now believe that the future of their children will be different. Wherever we went in the grassroots communities of rural India, there is an enormous emphasis on the education of children and the learning of new skills. That was true even of tribal families. They are convinced that their children will be able to enjoy a higher standard of life through education. Their ambition for their children's education had far outpaced the facilities that were available to them. Still, some of them did travel by buses, picked up more education and new skills, and fulfilled their parents' dreams. In Anaval, an adivasi village, more than 80 students went out every morning to nearby high schools and colleges to receive education. In 1998, the Anaval village milk cooperative contributed Rs.50,000 (U.S.$1,111) to building a high school in the village with dairy technology as one of its subjects. In these villages milk, and income from milk, have created hope for the future.

The Surat and Valsad milk unions, along with many other successful ones, have spawned grassroots leaders who possess the energy and vision required to diversify into additional ventures.

Such leaders have so much to offer and only a portion is consumed by the milk cooperatives. Normally, these leaders begin working with the visiting dairy personnel first, and then go to the top leadership of the union for more assignments and more areas to cover. At times, the union leadership is overwhelmed and does not want to be bothered by these energetic grassroots leaders. At other times, they are put on committees so that a part of their energy is consumed by trying to convince others. But if they survive those cooling off rounds, then they may, just may, get a sympathetic audience. But if there are social activists accompanying them from the region then everything changes. The combination of energetic grassroots leaders and social activists has resulted in practical ideas on biogas, health, hygiene, drinking water, irrigation, educational institutions, developmental projects and expenses, income generating schemes, and so on. The "milk only" policy goes against the huge groundswell of grassroots energy that the cooperatives have generated.

Once a grassroots leadership emerges with some amount of encouragement from the regional social activists, or from the union staff, their milk cooperatives want to explore the possibility of going beyond milk. Success in running a milk cooperative is often encouragement to do more. Those involved, and those who benefit most from the accomplishments in the dairying industry, want to fly, on the wings of their success in milk, to ventures beyond milk.

This has started happening in villages of Bihar and Rajasthan, the two states not known for economic development and/or a good administration. The impact of successful milk cooperatives, where not much else has succeeded, has galvanized their grassroots communities. Since they do not get much response from their politicians and administrators, they latch on to milk union personnel to help them in other fields as well. During our period of observation, the villagers repeatedly questioned the union personnel: "how long do you want us to wait?" Their other comments are much more telling: "why do you want to punish us just because our politicians and bureaucrats are no good?" That the milk cooperatives have succeeded in their grassroots communities, despite several problems created by politicians and bureaucrats, shows that they will succeed in other fields as well, provided they are given help and direction similar to that they received in cooperative dairying. The success in Kolhapur inspired the region to concentrate on women and their empowerment and, in that process, socially rejuvenate the rural society that sustains the milk cooperatives.

IV.   New Horizons

Venturing beyond milk is an undertaking that involves either the socially concerned directors of milk unions and their staff, or grassroots communities and their leadership. If there are significant accomplishments, then they get a mention in one of the NDDB's in-house journals. Further, if they are lucky, some scholar will study their achievements and write about them in national and international journals. We are of the opinion that the important theme of "going beyond milk" has yet to receive the attention that it deserves.

As students of development studies, we have felt that while milk cooperatives started off as something which was only about milk, in their sheer impact they certainly have gone much beyond it. And this calls for careful explorations, both by policy makers and the scholarly community, into where its impact has been felt. If the cooperatives have set into motion certain dynamics, can those dynamics be put to further use for areas in addition to milk?

We have watched some rural communities in Gujarat, since before the full impact of milk cooperatives was registered. Their transformation in some respects has been most significant. Earlier, we had observed those communities as they became involved in India's democratic process. We observed those communities getting involved in general elections, panchayat elections, and in their day-to-day democratic decision-making processes. Their democratic processes often reflected the basic reality of Indian society: deep divisions on caste and, sometimes, religious lines. While they made some workable compromises across such divides, they, nevertheless, did not do much to eradicate those barriers.

But the scene inside the milk cooperatives, in those very same villages, was different. Milk cooperatives, as a means of livelihood, forced the fractured societies of rural India to forge a *new* cooperative community. In earlier published works we mentioned how the same people behave differently in deliberations within panchayats, on the one hand, and in milk cooperatives on the other (Somjee and Somjee 1978).

The question for us was whether this new cooperative community, which had emerged in almost every rural community where there were milk cooperatives, could be put to further use or not? So far, in most districts, this new cooperative community has been put to use for only one purpose, i.e., milk. It seemed evident that there was much more that this new cooperative community could accomplish. Therefore, its further uses should be explored.

So far, only isolated experiments have been attempted. Some have succeeded and others have not. If one considers all of the successful isolated experiments, a profile of the successful undertaking emerges, which could also be pursued by unions in other districts.

For instance, if we were to combine the glorious success of Amul together with the Tribhuvandas Foundation in rural health, Dudhsagar's attempt to make women co-members, Sumul's inclusion of the adivasis in the milk producing community, Vasudhara's attempt to hand over the majority of milk cooperatives to women and also help them build micro-saving and lending groups, and Father Berechi's attempt to pay attention to the education of children, then we have a composite picture of success in ventures beyond milk. Imagine villages of half the total number of districts in India, which have milk cooperatives and newly forged cooperative communities, simultaneously enjoying all these facilities? What a great achievement that would be!

In reality, apart from the Green Revolution, which ensured the feeding of the world's second largest population with plenty to spare, nothing in rural India has succeeded so effectively as did the "dairy revolution." And the very nature of its success has given rise to an additional moral responsibility for development in other areas. With the help of socially concerned staff, regional social activists, and grassroots leaders, we believe the dairy revolution can, and should, pave the way for a variety of social and economic improvements in India. Dr. Amrita Patel, the present chairperson of the NDDB, has the necessary background for launching a rural health service revolution to go beyond the dairy revolution. And she may yet pursue that goal with great effectiveness.

When exploring new horizons, the solid achievements of milk cooperatives of India should be put to further use. These achievements have already enhanced the economic, social, and human resources of the areas where the cooperatives have operated. Efficient animal resources have been created, new economic communities have been built across the fractured traditional society, and over 6 million members have been involved in the participatory processes of grassroots communities. Together these constitute the new social and human capital needed to solve many more problems.

While such a resource-building process has been quietly going on, the challenges of liberalization and globalization have also been putting the technocratic leadership of milk cooperatives to its severest test. Several experiments in grassroots communities, unions and the apex body such as the NDDB have evoked different responses. In addition there are new challenges that have been unleashed by the national and international economic forces. And while there is a broad agreement on protecting the cooperative structures that have been put in place, there is also a diversity of perception and judgment on what will effectively deal with those forces. We have had endless discussions with the leadership at various levels about these and other related matters. Everyone that we spoke to was groping for solutions. For such a range of challenges and problems, there were no simple solutions. At the same time everyone was looking for a head start with a margin of safety for a possible change in direction should that become necessary.

In contemporary India, pragmatically changing direction is not always easy. It took the country more than three decades, and endless hardship, to know that neither public ownership nor uncontrolled private enterprise could provide solutions to all its economic problems. The same is true of cooperative structures. Once a decision is taken, one way or the other, a lot of vested interests, bureaucratic resistance, and legal and political rationale develop round it. Together they make any pragmatic change in course, even within small cooperative structures, difficult.

So before a final decision can be made, the consequences have to be clearly understood in order to avoid future recriminations. The maturing process for any organization requires that crucial decisions should be taken in an atmosphere of shared responsibility and transparency. That is now the new challenge before the milk cooperatives of India.

NOTES

1 For details on the formation and impact of Amul, see Somjee and Somjee (1989).

2 This was corroborated in the 49th *Annual Report of Sabarkantha Jilla Sahkari Sangh*, Himatnagar, 1998-1999.

3 We were privileged to watch the growth of the scheme from day one. For details see Geeta Somjee (1989:74-81).

4 Data obtained from the milk cooperative in a village called Railia Falia, near Valsad.

5 The NDDB has recently asked for legislation that will turn cooperatives into companies. This will keep out bureaucrats and politicians.

BIBLIOGRAPHY

Ardener, Shirley, ed. 1978. *Defining Women: The Nature of Women in Society*. London: Croom Helm and Oxford University Women's Studies Association.

Banas Dairy. nd. "An Oasis in Desert." Ahmedabad: Darshan.

Bobb, Dilip. 1994. "Yearning for Order," *India Today*, February 15.

Haq, Mahbub ul. 1995. *Reflections on Human Development* Oxford: Oxford University Press.

Dreze, Jean and Amartya Sen. 1995. *India: Economic Development and Social Opportunity*. New Delhi: Oxford University Press.

Dugger, Celia. W. 2000. "India Tries To Reassess Its Measure For Poverty." *The New York Times*, October 8.

Haq, Mahbub ul. 1995. *Reflections on Human Development*. Oxford: Oxford University Press.

Henderson, Jeffrey and Richard P. Appelbaum, eds. 1992. *States and Development in the Pacific Rim*. New York: Sage.

Huntington, S.P. and Joan Nelson. 1987. *No Easy Choice: Public Participation in Developing Countries*. Cambridge, MA: Harvard University Press.

India Office of the Registrar General. 2001. *Provisional Population Totals,* April. New Delhi: India.

Kurien. V. 1996. "Amul 50th Anniversary Celebrations Address." In *Amul: The Taste of India. 50 Years of Milk & Health*. Anand, India: Anand Press.

Narayan, Jayaprakash. 1959. *A Plea for the Reconstruction of Indian Polity* Kashi: Akhil Bharat Seva Sangh Prakashan.

NDDB. 1991. *A Note on Cooperative Development, Vol. III*. Anand: NDDB.

_____. 1998. "Cooperative Development Program of Kaira District. Co-Operative Milk Producers' Union Ltd." Anand: NDDB. p.ii

_____. 1999. "The Agenda for the Future." *NDDB Newsmagzine Diary,* November, Vol. II, (6):3.

Rao, V.M. 1995. *Developing Agro Enterprises Among Farm Women*. Pune: Vaikunth Mehta National Institute of Cooperative Management p. 4.

Singh, Katar. 1996. *Amul: The Taste of India. 50 years of Milk and Health*. Anand: Anand Press.

Somjee, A.H. 1982. *Political Capacity in Developing Societies*. New York, NY: St. Martin's Press.

_____. 1982. "Techno-managerial and Politico-Managerial Classes in a Milk Cooperative of India." *Journal for Asian and African Studies* XVII(1-2).

_____. 1986. *Political Society in Developing Countries*. New York, NY: St. Martin's Press.

_____ and Geeta Somjee. 1978. "Cooperative Dairying and the Profiles of Social Change in India." *Economic Development and Cultural Change* 26(3):577-590.

_____ and Geeta Somjee. 1995. *Development Success in Asia Pacific: An Exercise in Normative-Pragmatic Balance*. London: Macmillan.

Somjee, Geeta. 1989. *Narrowing the Gender Gap*. London: Macmillan.

_____ and A.H. Somjee. 1989. *Reaching Out to the Poor*. London: Macmillan.

Streeten, Paul Patrick. 1994. *Stragies for Human Development: Global Poverty and Unemployment*. Copenhagen: Copenhagen Business School Press.

_____. 1998. "The Cheerful Pessimist: Gunnar Myrdal The Dissenter." *World Development* 26(3):539-50.

_____. 1995. *Thinking About Development*. Cambridge: Cambridge University Press.

Sumul Dairy. 1999. "A Brief Note about Sumul Dairy." Mimeograph. Surat: Sumul Dairy.

Samakhya. n.d. "Review of Cooperative Performance of Women's Dairy Cooperative in Andhra Pradesh." Report prepared for the Andhra Pradesh Dairy Development Cooperative Federation,

Hyderabad and New Delhi: Ford Foundation.

Sen, Amartya. 1988. "Authoritarianism vs. Cooperation: Perspectives on Population." *Frontline* New Delhi: *The Hindu Group of Publications.*

Sen, D. and D. Jhansi Rani. 1990. "Women in Dairying: A Case Study." *The Journal of Rural Development* 9:809-831.

Shah, Tushar et al. 1992. "Designs for Democracy: Building Energetic Farmer Organizations." Presented at IRMA Symposium on Management of Rural Cooperatives, Institute of Rural Management, Anand, India.

Sinha, Frances. 1999. "Opportunities for Women's Empowerment through Membership of Dairy Cooperative Societies." Presented at the Women's Empowerment Workshop, Anand, India.

Stackhouse, John. 1993. "How India's Women Wage War on Drink." *The Globe And Mail*, May 11.

Srinivasan, Viji. 1986. *Indian Women- A Study of their Role in the Dairy Movement.* New Delhi: Ford Foundation Publication.

The Economic Times of India, October 18, 1998.

The Hindu, October 16, 1998.

The World Bank Report. 1993. *The East Asian Miracle: Economic Growth and Policy.* Oxford: Oxford University Press.

Tribhuvandas Foundation. 2000. Annual Report. Anand, India: Tribhuvandas Foundation.

Vijaya, G.P. and P.R. Shankar Mohan. 1998. "Cooperative Development Program: Mehsana District Co-Operative Milk Producers Union Ltd." Anand: NDDB.

Wayangankar, Arun. 1994. "The Empowerment of Indian Women Dairy Farmers." M.A. Thesis, University of New Mexico, Albuquerque, New Mexico.

INDEX